Commando Dad:
Raw Recruits

About the Author

I'm an ex-Royal Engineer commando and in my six years of service, I served three tours in Norway, a tour in the jungles of Belize and six months in the mountains of Iraq as part of Operation Desert Storm. I cleared mines, tracked drug barons through the jungle and skied across crevasse-ridden ice fields. But none of this prepared me for my most challenging mission: for the past eleven years I have been a stay-at-home dad to my three troopers: Sam, Jude and Liberty.

I used all of my experiences to write a book for new dads called *Commando Dad: Basic Training*. It's a clear, concise manual offering straightforward advice on the practical skills needed to be an effective dad. It's the parenting equivalent of *Basic Battle Skills*, the no-nonsense field training guide issued to all soldiers in the British Army. It struck a chord with a lot of new dads. However, on the Commando Dad website forums there are a lot of dads-to-be looking for information and support and this gave me the inspiration to write *Commando Dad: Raw Recruits*. This is the book I wish I'd been issued with when I found out I was going to be a new dad. It will give you everything you need to know for the whole 266 days. And counting.

Commando Dad: Raw Recruits

NEIL SINCLAIR

First published in Great Britain in 2014 by Yellow Kite
An imprint of Hodder & Stoughton
An Hachette UK company

7

Illustrations © Matt Smith

Trade Paperback ISBN 978 1 444 78881 5
eBook ISBN 978 1 444 78883 9

Book design by Janette Revill
Typeset in Serifa BT

Printed and bound by Clays Ltd, Elcograf S.p.A.

Hodder & Stoughton policy is to use papers that are natural, renewable
and recyclable products and made from wood grown in sustainable forests.
The logging and manufacturing processes are expected to conform to the
environmental regulations of the country of origin.

Hodder & Stoughton Ltd
338 Euston Road
London NW1 3BH

www.hodder.co.uk

A percentage of the author's profits from this book will go to the following charities:

Acorns Children's Hospice Trust, a registered UK charity offering a network of care and
support for life-limited and life-threatened children and young people, and their families.

The National Memorial Arboretum, the UK's year-round centre for Remembrance, a
spiritually uplifting place that honours the fallen, recognises service and sacrifice, and fosters
pride in the country. The arboretum is part of the Royal British Legion family of charities.

Disclaimer

I have written this book based on my own experiences. Where I reference the health and safety of your CO or your BTs, I have had the text reviewed and approved by health care professionals to ensure that the information is accurate and in line with current thinking and practice at the time of publication. However, the publisher, author and experts disclaim any liability from any injury that may result from the use, proper or improper, of the information contained in this book. Guidance and guidelines on pregnancy and childbirth change constantly and *Commando Dad: Raw Recruits* should not be considered a substitute for the advice of your health care professional or your own common sense.

I would like to dedicate this book to my own unit.

To my wife, Tara: although our parenting adventures were always unplanned, they're still brilliant because we're having them together.

To Sam, Jude and Liberty: I love you very much and hope that you use the lessons we learned together when you bring your own troopers into this world.

Acknowledgements

Thanks to the following people, for their help in reviewing and approving content:

- Kate Bedding, Research and Education Consultant, LSA Auditor, NCT Antenatal Teacher, Preparation for Birth & Beyond Teacher & Postnatal Facilitator and Public Governor of Liverpool Women's NHS Foundation Trust Hospital, for reviewing the whole manuscript and being a constant source of support
- Mark Clement-Jones, Consultant Obstetrician, Liverpool Women's NHS Foundation Trust Hospital for reviewing the whole manuscript and making positive suggestions
- Andrea Smith, Midwife, Samuel Johnson Midwifery led unit, Lichfield for reviewing *Chapter 1: Raw Recruits: 266 days and counting, Chapter 2: Actions on: appointments, Chapter 7: What happens next, Chapter 8: When things don't go to plan* and *Chapter 10: Breaking the code* brilliantly, and at short notice
- The British Red Cross Society. The first aid information in the 'Emergency deployment' section of *Chapter 8: When things don't go to plan* has been approved by the British Red Cross Society
- Alix Henley and Judith Schott from Sands, the stillbirth and neonatal death charity, who helped with the section 'If your baby dies' in *Chapter 8: When things don't go to plan*
- Dr Gary Brickley, Senior Lecturer in Sports and Exercise Science at the University of Brighton; Chartered Scientist; British Association of Sport and Exercise Accredited scientist; and International coach for his help with Chapter 3: Fit for fatherhood
- Ian North, Development Manager, Dads4Dads for not only reviewing the young dads section, but also for helping me find dads that were willing to share their stories
- Stacey Wills, from the Twins and Multiple Births Association (TAMBA) for reviewing the sections on twins and multiples

Honour Roll

Thanks to the following dads, who responded to my 'Call to arms' for help with this book. They shared their experiences, offered advice, support, guidance, tips, and even provided some brilliant quotes.

Adam Baker
Andrew Brooker
Andy Long
Andy McKevitt
Calum Beatt
Chris Simpson
Christopher Jones
Dan Fuller
Daniel Saxton
Dave Boatwright
David Topping
Devlin Waddell
Devon Starmer
Ed Rankin
Edward Starmer
Grant Mills
Hywel Davies
Ian North
Jack Carter
James Fenwick
James Gibbs
James Heywood
James Waddell
James Wickham
Jamie Williams
Jennifer Gray
John Allen
Jon Watkins
Jon Wheale

Kevin S
Lee Parker
Lee Richardson
Leigh Greenwood
Liam D
Marc Topliss
Mark Baker
Mark Yates
Martin Scott
Matt Richards
Matthew Walker-Rowe
Neil Mawson
Neil White
Nick Burbidge
Nick Dawson
Paul Drake
Paul Hope
Philip Sowerby
Rich Brown
Rob Falls
Ron Murray
Sam Winterson
Stephen Ellis
Steve Cooper
Stuart Cooper
Tony Barnett
Tony Ewart
William Adams

Contents

Contents

Foreword

In today's society, dads are actively encouraged to bond with their babies while they are still in the womb and to be at the birth, acting as birth companions and offering support and encouragement to their partners throughout labour. But where do they get the skills to do this? Where do they have the opportunity to find out about what is going to happen to their partner and therefore how they can be most effective? How do they know what to expect when they see their partner in pain, or what to do when they bring their baby home from the hospital?

While there is an overwhelming amount of information on pregnancy and labour that can be accessed through books, forums and the media, the majority is aimed at mums, or couples in general, not specifically at dads. As someone who works with fathers I am continually aware of the need to make it relevant for them, to ensure that they are receiving the information that they need and that they have the opportunity to discuss the things that concern *them*.

I am therefore delighted that Commando Dad has used his winning formula of combining concise information, real-life experience, illustrations and summaries to cover all the essential topics related to pregnancy, birth and those first few weeks in this outstanding book. The number of subjects that he has managed to cover, and in such detail, ensures that this is one book no dad can afford to be without.

Those who work with dads know that if couples have the opportunity to make informed choices throughout pregnancy and during birth, they are better able to adjust to becoming parents. Commando Dad has provided all the essential information dads (and mums) need to make those choices.

Dads, I recommend you use the chapters in this book as the basis for discussions with your partner about the choices that are available to you as a couple: for example, where do you want your baby to be born?

To deliberate over the types of pain management available and to know in advance of deployment day what your partner might want – or not want! To think and then discuss together how your lives are going to change as individuals and as a couple, and what you might feel at meeting your baby for the first time.

And with only 266 days to prepare for this life-changing experience, there is not a moment to lose. I recommend you start reading immediately!

Raw Recruits is simply the most essential bit of kit for all dads-to-be, whether they are expecting their first or third baby.

Kate Bedding

BA (Hons), M.Res, PGDip, PGCE, Diploma Postnatal Facilitation NCT, Diploma Antenatal Education NCT, PhD student (Midwifery – UCLAN)

Introduction

TO ALL DADS TO BE (henceforth known as Commando Dads)

This book has been written for YOU.

When I first found out that I was going to be a dad, I felt a lot of emotions, the main one of which was definitely fear. We weren't trying to start a family – we hadn't even been thinking about it. I'd only been married eighteen months. None of my friends were dads. I'd never even held a baby. And yet in less than 266 days, I was going to be a dad.

Gentlemen, I don't use the word 'fear' lightly. As a commando I experienced truly frightening situations. I soon realised that I didn't fear being a dad – that was now inevitable – I feared the unknown.

I wanted to get educated in the basics as fast as the situation demanded. I wanted to know what was going to physically happen to my wife (mums-to-be are henceforth known as COs or Commanding Officers); I wanted to know what I could do to help; I wanted to know the practicalities of pregnancy – appointments and scans and classes; I wanted to know about labour.

The books that were available focussed exclusively on this kind of mental preparation via huge amounts of detailed information. Although the content was essential, there was so much of it that it was overwhelming – I suffered sensory overload. Also, having been through pregnancy and childbirth with my CO, I now know that mental preparation is only part of the story. Men also need to be physically and emotionally prepared.

The manual that you are holding in your hands will provide you with clear and concise guidance on what to expect from the moment you find out you're going to be a dad until the moment your baby trooper deploys. It will help to mentally, physically and emotionally prepare you for fatherhood, but it will not saturation bomb you with information.

Although your CO alone is facing the intense demands of pregnancy and childbirth, do not feel you have no place. That would be to fundamentally misunderstand your role as a dad. It starts now. You need to be essential backup support to your CO – she needs you. You need to provide physical support when she is tired; emotional support when she is feeling down; and mental support when she is perhaps overwhelmed or fearful. This will help pave the way for a new little life that you have helped to create. What you do from this point forwards really counts. This book will help.

A prepared Commando Dad

How to use *Commando Dad: Raw Recruits*

Commando Dad: Raw Recruits is your essential coursebook for nine months. It supports your active participation in the pregnancy and childbirth process. Keep it close and refer to it often.

The book is supported by the Commando Dad website, where you will find extra resources, helpful 'how to' videos and forums, where dads can provide you with help, support and advice on every question you need to ask. There is no such thing as a stupid question. As you gain skills, experience and confidence, I would ask that you remain on the forums to help other Commando Dads as they do their bit to swell the ranks. Please log on to find out what's available: www.commandodad.com.

Throughout *Commando Dad: Raw Recruits* I use the following terms:

- CO: your Commanding Officer – the person in charge – i.e. the mum-to-be
- BT: your baby trooper

I have also included quotes from new dads, in the 'Advice from the front line' sections. All of these dads use the Commando Dad forums, and responded to a call for action to help dads-to-be, just like you.

The journey that you are now on is an inherently emotional one. You will probably already know this because of how you felt when you found out that you were going to be a dad. For me, the main response was fear, but other new dads have told me they've felt anguish, awe, contentment, excitement, fear, gratitude, joy, panic, relief, shock, wonder and worry. And they're just the ones I've spoken to. Throughout pregnancy, there are significant milestones that may trigger huge emotional responses and to make you aware of these, I have created 'Emotion alerts' throughout the book. I am not telling you what emotions to feel and when. You may find that you feel very emotional throughout the whole nine months or that you feel very little emotion until your BT deploys. There is no right or wrong way to be feeling.

Where I want to draw your attention to something that may require urgent medical assistance, I have used the heading 'Call the medic'. For things that may require medical assistance, I have used the heading 'Medic: stand by'. For more information about conditions that require urgent medical attention, and pregnancy complications, see *Chapter 4: Call the medic.*

Throughout the book I refer to you and your CO going to hospital to give birth. This is because it is the most common place for births to happen. If you and your CO choose to use a birthing centre, a home birth or an alternative, a lot of the information in the book is still relevant to you. Please also see *Chapter 9: Special ops.*

RECAP AND REFRESH

I have worked hard to ensure that I cover a lot of information in this book and at the end of every chapter I have included a brief summary of the main topics covered and signposted where you can find other information that may be relevant to you.

COMMANDO DAD GOLDEN RULES

Below you will find five golden rules that will stand you in good stead for the next 266 days. They will also lay the foundations for the elite standards you will be working towards and operating at, as a new dad:

1 A Commando Dad knows preparation and planning prevent poor parental performance. Get ready. Now. Get as much information as you can; if there is anything you don't understand, ask

2 A Commando Dad knows when to ask for and accept help – both for himself and his CO

3 A Commando Dad is a problem solver. In any given situation he will improvise, adapt and overcome

4 A Commando Dad keeps calm under pressure

5 A Commando Dad takes care of his unit with all the means at his disposal

Raw Recruits: 266 days and counting

1

THE BRIEF
Less than 266 days separate you from fatherhood. A period of massive physical – and potentially emotional – change lies ahead for your CO as your BT is created, grows and develops. Arm yourself now with essential information about the changes that lie ahead. Planning and preparation prevent poor parental performance.

THE OBJECTIVE
Every BT develops differently and no two COs experience pregnancy in the same way. But by the end of this chapter you will have an overview of the physical changes that your CO will undergo over the next nine months – from conception to deployment. You will understand how the growth of your BT impacts her body and have an overview of your BT's development.

ADVICE FROM THE FRONT LINE

'I was a hands-on dad from day one. It was all about looking after the wife and making sure she had everything she needed – from food to sleep. It was all about her and the unborn! Some fellas are not prepared for this or the ups and downs (which happen a lot), but as we worked as a team we were able to manage this and it made us stronger.'

PAUL HOPE

EMOTION ALERT

Your fatherhood journey starts here. While it is not going to be a physical one – at least not for the next nine months – be aware that it may be an emotional one. When you find out that you're going to be a dad, you can't help but analyse your experiences with your own dad and start drawing conclusions. Maybe you didn't have a father figure in your life and wonder if that will affect your ability to be a good dad; maybe you had a fantastic dad and wonder if you will ever be able to be as good as he was with your own troopers; maybe your dad's fathering skills left a lot to be desired and you're worried that you may make the same mistakes. While I can't talk to these maybes, I can tell you a definite: the only person who has any control over what kind of dad you'll be is you. So decide to be the best dad you can be. This starts by supporting your CO now.

She may be feeling anxious about becoming a parent, but she also has soaring pregnancy hormones to deal with. These will have physical and emotional effects. Anticipate that she may have mood swings, especially in the early days. You may find that you are bearing the brunt of these rapidly changing emotions, but try not to take it personally.

Your CO is on an emotional rollercoaster. Be there and reassure her that everything is OK. Mood swings should start to stabilise after around twelve weeks.

TERMS USED IN THE MONTH BY MONTH BREAKDOWN

TRIMESTERS
Your CO's pregnancy is split into three parts, or trimesters. Different practitioners may use different markers to determine the start and end dates of each trimester. The most common division is as follows:
- **First trimester:** 2–13 weeks
  - Your CO is considered to be two weeks into her pregnancy when fertilisation occurs. As it is impossible to predict the moment of conception, it is counted from a date that is known, i.e. the start of her last period
- **Second trimester:** 14–26 weeks
- **Third trimester:** 27–40 weeks

SYMPTOMS
Below I have included some possible symptoms that your CO may experience throughout her pregnancy. The month I have put them in is to indicate when this symptom may first appear. In reality she may experience none of these symptoms, or experience them all throughout all of her pregnancy, or experience them at different times. Every pregnancy is different.

WEIGHT GAIN
The average weight gain for a CO over the course of a pregnancy is 25–35 lb (11–16 kg), broken down as follows:
- BT: 8 lb (4 kg)
- Placenta: 2–3 lb (1–1.4 kg)
- Amniotic fluid: 2–3 lb (1–1.4 kg)
- Breast tissue: 2–3 lb (1–1.4 kg)

- Blood supply: 4 lb (2 kg)
- Stored fat for delivery and breastfeeding: 5–9 lb (2.2–4 kg)
- Larger uterus: 2–5 lb (1–2.2 kg)

But weight gain will be dependent on a number of factors, including your CO's body shape and weight going into pregnancy. Your CO will need to speak to her doctor or midwife, who can provide tailored advice about her weight gain. For this reason, I haven't included any weight gain information in the tables below. See *Chapter 3: Fit for fatherhood* for advice on healthy eating during pregnancy that ensures you, your CO – and your BT – have the nourishment you need.

 ADVICE FROM THE FRONT LINE

'The CO will be going through a huge number of changes – physically and emotionally – so be there to support her, reassure her and tell her that everything will be all right.'

CALUM BEATT

MONTH 1 (weeks 2–4)

FIRST TRIMESTER
Life begins
A short, but miraculously busy month.

Your BT
- Size: a pinhead by month end
- Your BT is a ball of cells that is dividing into three layers that will later form organs and tissues

- The placenta is functioning, but will continue to develop and perform more complex tasks

Your CO

Possible physical changes
None

Possible symptoms	Possible cause
Missed or abnormal period	A shorter or lighter 'period' may actually be caused by a fertilised egg burrowing into the lining of her uterus
Morning sickness (despite the misleading name it can last all day)	No definitive answer, but it is thought that fluctuating pregnancy hormones are the culprit

MEDIC: STAND BY
Call your medical support team if your CO's morning sickness never goes away, if she is vomiting several times a day, loses weight and feels dizzy and faint. This could be a condition called hyperemesis gravidarum that requires medical assistance.

MONTH 2 (weeks 5–8)

FIRST TRIMESTER
Critical development commences

Your BT
- Size: pinhead to 1.3 cm
- The following begin to form:
  - The digestive tract – stomach and intestines
  - The sensory organs – eyes, ears, tongue, transparent skin and nose
  - The neural tube – brain, spinal cord and other nerve tissue
  - The respiratory system – lungs
  - The circulatory system – blood and heart, that begins to beat
  - Limb buds – that will eventually become arms, together with distinguishable feet and hands
  - Tooth buds, palate and tongue
  - Muscle and bone

TOP TIP

COMMANDO DAD TOP TIP
You and your CO are in this together. If you're not already, you both need to adopt a healthy lifestyle: eating well, no drinking and no smoking. Getting fit or maintaining fitness levels is also good for both of you. See *Chapter 3: Fit for fatherhood* for more information.

ADVICE FROM THE FRONT LINE
'When it comes to the CO, do not complain about anything. Nothing you are experiencing, either physically or emotionally, comes close to pregnancy. If you ever forget this, you will be reminded in short order.'
JOHN ALLEN

Your CO

Possible physical changes	Possible causes
Thickening waistline	Your CO's uterus is growing in size
Larger breasts	Preparation for breastfeeding (see below)
Longer and thicker hair than usual	Thought to occur because of pregnancy hormones

Possible symptoms	Possible cause
Increased fatigue	Your CO's body is working overtime to create your BT. Soaring progesterone levels can make her sleepy, while lower blood sugar levels, lower blood pressure and increased blood production can increase the feelings of tiredness
Dizziness	Lower blood pressure might cause light-headedness or dizziness, but also hunger or fatigue
Sensitive breasts	Fluctuating hormones – oestrogen and progesterone – and growth of the breasts to prepare for breastfeeding. The fat layer in them thickens, milk glands multiply, and blood flow increases
Increased urination, and sometimes leaking urine when sneezing, coughing or laughing	Blood volume is increased and so kidneys are working harder. As the pregnancy progresses, the growing uterus will increasingly put pressure on the bladder

Blocked or runny nose	Thought to occur because pregnancy hormones, specifically oestrogen, effect the mucous membranes in your CO's nose
Food cravings and/or aversions Heightened sense of smell	Not conclusive, but extreme hormonal changes are thought to have a huge impact on taste and smell
Mood swings	Fluctuating hormone levels and anxiety caused by going through an intense period of change
Heartburn Constipation	Progesterone relaxing the muscle that keeps food in the stomach (the gastroesophageal sphincter) and/or food staying in your CO's stomach longer. This gives the food more time to be absorbed into her bloodstream, maximising the nutrition that your BT can take from it

TOP TIP

COMMANDO DAD TOP TIP

Increased urination may make your CO inclined to drink less. However, she'll need to keep hydrated, but should best avoid diuretics like tea or coffee, which will just exacerbate the problem. Water is a great choice.

ADVICE FROM THE FRONT LINE

'In terms of backup support, just be there for your CO and listen. Her body is going through massive changes – yours is not!'

SAM WINTERSON

MONTH 3 (weeks 9–13)

FIRST TRIMESTER
BT fully forms – fine-tuning of physiology begins

Your BT

- Size: 1.8–6.7 cm crown (i.e. top) of head to rump, or bottom
- Twelve weeks after your CO's last period, your BT is fully formed, with organs, muscles, limbs and bones in place; they just need to grow and mature.
- The following are now formed:
  - Arms
  - Hands
  - Feet and toes (and fingerprints)
  - Skin – but it is still transparent
  - Vital organs – liver, kidneys, intestines, brain and lungs – are functional
  - The circulatory and urinary systems are formed and now performing more complex tasks, and the liver produces bile and red blood cells
  - Placenta

- The following begin to form:
  - Face
  - Genitals. Sex can't be determined yet, although sex organs are well developed
  - Neurological connections in the brain (synapses)
- BT becomes active: swallowing fluid, opening and closing hands, kicking limbs. These movements can be detected by ultrasound

Your CO

Possible physical changes	Possible causes
Linea nigra – a brown line of pigmentation between the bellybutton and the pubic bone may appear (sometimes it may extend further up the abdomen)	Pregnancy hormones cause a darkening of the skin. It will fade after the birth.
Hair, fingernails and toes are growing faster	Pregnancy hormones and multivitamins
Oily skin and/or acne	Pregnancy hormones causing increased blood flow and oil production (which causes the pregnancy 'glow')

Possible symptoms	Possible causes
Problems sleeping	A number of reasons: more vivid dreams, discomfort of pregnancy symptoms and possible anxiety about pregnancy

MONTH 4 (weeks 14–17)

SECOND TRIMESTER
Rapid growth begins

Your BT
- Size: 8–11 cm crown of head to rump
- The following are now formed:
  - Facial features: your BT can squint, frown, grimace, yawn and pull faces
  - Eyelids, eyebrows, eyelashes, nails and hair
  - Fingers and unique fingerprints. Your BT may suck their thumb
  - Toes
  - Lungs – your BT is now inhaling and exhaling the amniotic fluid they're immersed in
  - Circulatory and urinary systems
  - Genitals. Sex can now be determined with an ultrasound scan
- The following continue to form:
  - Your BT's skeleton. It's mostly pliable tissue, cartilage, but it will gradually harden throughout pregnancy, apart from the head, which will need to remain pliable so that it will be able to pass through your CO's birth canal during labour
- Teeth and bones become denser
  - The following begin to form:
  - Hair on head, eyebrows and eyelashes
  - Fat, which will help your BT's heat production and metabolism
  - Sweat glands

Your CO

Possible physical changes	Possible causes
A more obvious baby bump	A growing uterus that can no longer be hidden. Skin, muscle and ligaments begin to stretch
Breasts leak a small amount of milk	Your CO is producing colostrum or 'first milk'

Possible symptoms	Possible causes
Fluttering movements inside ('quickening')	Your CO can feel your BT moving
Less frequent urination	Your CO's uterus is shifting
Nosebleeds and/or more noticeable veins	Your CO's blood volume is increasing
Increased energy and appetite	The side effects that your CO experienced in the first trimester may start to subside
Heartburn	Thought to occur because the pregnancy hormone progesterone (that relaxes the muscles of your CO's uterus) may relax the valve that separates her oesophagus from her stomach. Later in the pregnancy, heartburn will be caused by a large uterus pushing your CO's stomach and intestines upwards

MONTH 5 (weeks 18–21)

SECOND TRIMESTER
Midway: your BT is very active

Your BT

- Size: 12cm crown of head to rump and 27 cm head to heel. From around twenty weeks your BT's legs are no longer tightly curled up, making it possible to measure from head to heel
- The following are now formed:
  - Reflexes: your BT would suck if their lips were stroked, can swallow and get hiccups (silent though, as there's no air in their throat)
- The following continue to form:
  - The nerve cells serving each of the senses – taste, smell, hearing, seeing and touch – are developing in their specialised areas of the brain
  - Taste: your BT's taste buds are beginning to develop and they can distinguish sweet from bitter tastes
  - Hearing: your BT can now hear your CO's voice (and perhaps yours), her heart, her stomach rumbling and growling, as well as sounds outside her body. One of the reasons your BT will find you saying 'shh' so calming when they deploy is because it reminds them of the sound of your CO's blood pumping through her veins
  - Seeing: your BT's retinas are sensitive to light
  - Skin (still transparent). Blood vessels are visible through it
  - Meconium forms from materials ingested in the uterus. It will appear in their nappy after birth and for the first 2–3 days as a very sticky, dark green poo
- The following begin to form:
  - Vernix caseosa, a waxy substance that protects your BT's skin from amniotic fluid and keeps it supple
  - Fat, which your BT needs to keep warm

Your CO

Possible physical changes	Possible causes
Obviously pregnant	
No waist	Your CO's uterus moves up out of her pelvis
Tiny red marks on the face, shoulders and arms	Dilated blood vessels

Possible symptoms	Possible causes
Lower abdominal aches and pains	Physical changes as the uterus continues to grow
Increased sweating	Increased activity in the thyroid gland

MONTH 6 (weeks 22–26)

SECOND TRIMESTER
Intense brain development

Your BT
- Size: 28–36 cm crown of head to heel
- The following are now formed:
  - Eyes, which are now open, but they don't have any colour yet
  - Taste buds
- The following continue to form:
  - Fat
  - The pancreas – essential to producing hormones
  - Lungs, to prepare for breathing
  - Brain

- • Patterns of sleeping and waking
- The following begin to form:
  - • Lanugo, a very fine, soft hair that covers your BT's paper-thin skin. Your BT will begin to shed this shortly before birth

Your CO

Possible physical changes	Possible causes
Belly-button pops out	Your CO's expanding uterus pushes her abdomen forward
Stretch marks on abdomen, buttocks, breasts and thighs	Rapid growth and stretching of your CO's skin
Increased vaginal discharge	Your CO's body increases discharge to help prevent infection

Possible symptoms	Possible causes
Changes to eyes: dry, sore, red or watery	Sometimes called 'Dry eye syndrome' – thought to occur because of a drop in your CO's male hormones
Achy, burning or tingly fingers, wrists and hands	Carpal tunnel syndrome: fluid retention and swelling can increase the pressure in the carpal tunnel (or passageway) in your CO's wrist, pinching the nerve that runs through it
Feeling/being off balance	Your CO's centre of gravity has now shifted
Itchy skin	Rapid growth and stretching of your CO's skin

MEDIC: STAND BY
Call your medical support team if your CO has vaginal discharge that is discoloured or smells strange or if she feels itchy. She may have an infection.

MONTH 7 (weeks 27–30)

THIRD TRIMESTER
Central nervous system and organs mature

Your BT
- Growth lengthwise slows. Size: 36–40 cm crown of head to heel
- Your BT may begin to turn this month to be head down (ready for birth)
- The following are now formed:
  - Senses: your BT will now react to sound and light
  - Rhythmic breathing patterns
  - The ability to regulate body temperature
- The following continue to form:
  - The respiratory system
  - The digestive tract
  - Brain tissue and a larger head to accommodate the brain
  - Skeleton
  - Fat

Your CO

Possible symptoms	Possible causes
Leg cramps	Thought to occur because of the extra weight your CO is carrying or her growing uterus restricting her blood circulation. Diet may also be a factor
Mildly swollen ankles, feet and fingers	Your CO's body is holding more water than usual, and as the day wears on, it gathers in the lowest parts of her body. It is exacerbated by hot weather or if she is spending a lot of time on her feet
Varicose veins Haemorrhoids	The weight of your BT is pressing on the large blood vessels in your CO's pelvis and hormone changes affecting blood vessels can slow the return of blood to her heart. This causes smaller veins in the pelvis, legs and rectum to swell
Shortness of breath	Your CO's uterus is now pushing against her diaphragm
Increased urination	Caused by your CO's uterus pushing against her bladder

CALL THE MEDIC

Get your CO emergency medical assistance if she has sudden or severe swelling in her face, hands or feet. This could indicate pre-eclampsia, potentially a very serious condition.

MONTH 8 (weeks 31–35)

THIRD TRIMESTER
Home stretch: BT gains weight rapidly as they prepare for labour

YOUR BT

- Size: 40–46 cm crown of head to heel
- The following are now formed:
    - Your BT's body is now all in proportion
    - Hearing
    - Finger and toenails
    - Kidneys
    - Pigment in their eyes: your BT has blue eyes, although this may later change

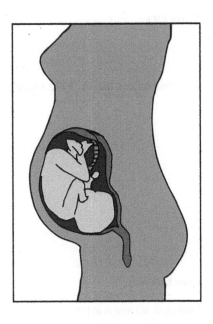

- The following continue to form:
    - Fat: your BT will gain about half a pound every week until week 38 and will become less wrinkly as they fill out
    - Lungs
    - Liver
    - Skeleton: their skeleton continues to harden, but their head remains pliable to enable it to pass through your CO's birth canal. Soft spots – or fontanelles – will remain on your BT's head for up to eighteen months before their skull fully fuses together
    - Immune system

TOP TIP

COMMANDO DAD TOP TIP
Do not worry about touching your BT's fontanelle, or soft spot, when they're deployed. Although the skull is not fully fused, their brain isn't exposed in any way. A thick, protective membrane is what actually puts the 'soft' in soft spot.

Your CO

Possible physical symptoms	Possible causes
A different walking gait, more like a waddle	Your CO's centre of balance has shifted to accommodate her growing uterus, and as labour approaches her pelvic joints will loosen ready for labour. Together, these will make your CO unstable. This causes muscle strain and can cause your BT to waddle. This may be even more pronounced when your BT drops into your CO's pelvis (see page 26)

Possible symptoms	Possible causes
Lower back pain	Strain on your CO's body and/or poor posture
Tingling or numbness in the pelvic region	Thought to be caused by the pelvic joints loosening, ready for labour
Pelvic pain, which may make it difficult for your CO to get around	Pelvic girdle pain or symphysis pubis dysfunction is caused by a misalignment or stiffness of your CO's pelvic joints at either the back or front of her pelvis. It is common, but the severity varies widely. Your CO should speak to her midwife or doctor to discuss treatment and techniques to manage the pain and discomfort

| Braxton Hicks contractions: your CO's uterus hardens and contracts | Your CO's body is beginning to practise for labour, but these type of contractions do not open the cervix and therefore they are completely safe. When they last for a long time and/or feel intense, they are sometimes described as 'false labour' |

TOP TIP

COMMANDO DAD TOP TIP

Once your BT is 37 weeks, they are considered full term. See 'How to recognise labour' in *Chapter 6: Deployment day*.

MONTH 9 (weeks 36–40)

THIRD TRIMESTER
Rapid weight gain as your BT prepares for labour

ADVICE FROM THE FRONT LINE

'I guess the most important thing any Commando Dad can do for his CO is to just be there. Whether it's a shoulder rub or making a cuppa, just be there. It's not just about earning Brownie Points – it really makes you feel like you've done something to help.'

DAVE BOATWRIGHT

Your BT

- Size: 47–51 cm crown of head to heel
- The following are now fully formed:
  - All organ systems
  - Brain
  - Lungs
  - The skeleton is hardened (excluding the head)
  - Muscles: arm and leg muscles are strong (as your CO will know from feeling your BT move around)
  - Reflexes are now fully coordinated so they can blink, turn their head, grasp firmly
- Lanugo, the fine hair that covered your baby, begins to be shed, though some may remain at birth on the baby's shoulders, folds of skin and backs of ears

Your CO

Possible physical symptoms	Possible causes
Breasts begin to leak	Your CO is producing colostrum, or 'first milk'

Possible symptoms	Possible cause
Less indigestion Improved breathing Increased urination Back pain	Your BT, who is now head down, will 'drop' into your CO's pelvis. This is called 'lightening'. It may give her a heavier feeling in her pelvis, but less pressure just below her ribcage will make it easier to breathe and eat, without getting indigestion
Frustration	Your CO will now be very large, uncomfortable and eager to go into labour

ADVICE FROM THE FRONT LINE

'Everyone (and their dog) is only too willing to give you advice during and after the pregnancy – and no two pieces are the same. In the end I had an auto response, "Thanks, that's very interesting and I will bear that in mind". The bottom line is that no two pregnancies are the same and everyone is different – the worst thing I did was try and compare our's to other people's. I probably spent too much time on the internet reading about what could go wrong instead of concentrating on how amazing it all was.' CALUM BEATT

RECAP AND REFRESH

Chapter 1: Raw Recruits has provided:
- A general overview of:
  - The physical changes that your CO may experience
  - Your BT's development
- Information about symptoms that you shouldn't ignore, and when it's necessary to call the medic. For a more detailed overview about what physical symptoms are normal, and which ones aren't, including how to recognise potentially serious problems, both physical (e.g. pre-eclampsia) and mental (e.g. antenatal depression), please go to *Chapter 4: Call the medic*
- There is more information about antenatal scans and appointments in *Chapter 2: Actions on appointments*
- If you and your CO are expecting twins or multiples, you can find

additional information about antenatal scans and appointments in the 'Multiple deployments' section of *Chapter 9: Special ops*

* It is essential that you both have the healthiest lifestyle possible. Starting now. Find more information, tips and advice in *Chapter 3: Fit for fatherhood*

Actions on appointments

2

THE BRIEF

Antenatal appointments are a crucial element of pregnancy. They provide you with an essential contact with the medical support team – your midwife, doctors and sonographers – that is going to help you and your CO through pregnancy and childbirth. Books can provide you with general information about pregnancy; your medical support team can provide specific answers to your questions about *your* CO and BT. Where possible, attend.

THE OBJECTIVE

By the end of this chapter, you'll have an overview of the antenatal appointments that your CO will be invited to attend throughout pregnancy. It also provides information about antenatal classes: what they are, what's available and how to access them. There is also a section on paternity leave and pay, what it is, who is eligible and how to apply.

ADVICE FROM THE FRONT LINE

'Time spent in reconnaissance is seldom wasted.'
NICK BURBIDGE

'Try and get to all the appointments if you can. During pregnancy your CO can become ... let's just say "not themselves", but if you're there you can make sure you ask the questions you want answers to. Plus it will help you start on the road to bonding with your new baby.'
DAN SAXTON

What you need to know:

- In a single pregnancy with no complications, your CO will receive eight to ten appointments and two to three scans:
  - A 'booking appointment' at 8–12 weeks, followed by appointments at:
    - 16 weeks
    - 25 weeks
    - Every three weeks until 34 weeks (weeks 28, 31 and 34)
    - Every other week or so after 34 weeks (weeks 36, 38, 41 or thereabouts)
    - 41 weeks if your BT hasn't deployed
  - Scans typically occur at:
    - 8–14 weeks. This is the 'dating scan' where you will see your BT for the first time and be given a reliable date for when they may deploy
    - 18–22 weeks. This is the 'anomaly scan' to confirm that your BT is developing normally
- In certain circumstances your CO may require more scans, such as:
  - Your CO is considered to be at a higher risk of complications

- Your CO is expecting twins or multiples. Please see *Chapter 9: Special ops* for more information about appointments for these multiple deployments
- Your employer is not required by law to give you time away from work to attend these appointments. However, it might be worth a chat with your manager or HR department to see if they are willing, or able, to let you attend appointments. Read below to see what each scan and appointment involves so that if you can only attend some, you can make an informed choice about which ones would work best for you both
- Appointments will not only give you and your CO information about maintaining a healthy pregnancy, but also an opportunity to ask questions

 COMMANDO DAD TOP TIP

You may not be able to attend all appointments, but let your CO know she's still got your support. Call or send a supportive text on the day to let her know you're thinking of her.

ADVICE FROM THE FRONT LINE

'From the start the biggest benefit I found was to involve myself in everything I could. If you don't, you very quickly start to feel left out when things are mentioned and you don't have a clue what they are talking about. I managed to get to every midwife/doctor appointment and scans. My boss and company were very flexible about this.'

PAUL DRAKE

ANTENATAL APPOINTMENTS AND SCANS

Although there is a set of scheduled appointments and scans, you or your CO can contact your midwife and doctor at any time if you have any worries or concerns.

Informing your doctor or a midwife

When your CO finds out she is pregnant, she will need to let her doctor or a midwife know, so that she can immediately gain access to the care she needs and can have the first official antenatal appointment (the booking appointment) scheduled.

This initial contact will enable her to receive information about how to take care of herself and her BT through diet and lifestyle choices. Your CO will need to tell the doctor if:

- She has pre-existing medical conditions, including diabetes and high blood pressure
- If anyone in either of your families has previously had a BT with a congenital defect, such as spina bifida
- If there is a history in either of your families of an inherited disease, for example, sickle cell or cystic fibrosis

TOP TIP

COMMANDO DAD TOP TIP

Your CO will need to go to this visit with a full bladder, as the doctor will want to confirm her pregnancy with their own test, which is more often than not a urine test. However, some surgeries may prefer to give a blood test.

ADVICE FROM THE FRONT LINE

'We told close family quite early, but only after CO had a test at the doctor's. I don't know why, but for some reason having a doctor tell us made it more real, even

> *though as we are both engineers, we understand that the science in the home tests is essentially the same as what the doctors do'.*
> PHILIP SOWERBY

FIRST APPOINTMENT: Booking appointment
Eight to 12 weeks

This is a very busy appointment that involves filling in a lot of paperwork. The 'booking' refers to booking your CO in for maternity care offered by your local healthcare trust. This appointment could be with your GP or, more likely, a midwife. The midwife could be attached to your local hospital or your doctor's surgery or she could be a community midwife. Depending on what's available in your local area, this booking appointment could be held at the hospital, your local midwife-led unit, at your doctor's surgery or in your home.

This is your midwife's opportunity to get to know your CO and family history (for both of you). She will use this information to determine the level of care for your CO and whether she needs additional support from a consultant obstetrician or a specialist midwife.

Your CO will get asked about:
- **The date of her last period.** This is an indicator of your CO's due date. See 'Dating scan' (page 37) for more information about the scan that will be able to more accurately predict the date your BT will deploy
- **Previous miscarriages and abortions.**
- **Family history.** This may – or may not – have a bearing on your pregnancy. Your CO will be advised of screening tests for conditions and given information to allow you both to make a balanced judgement about whether to take them or not

- **Age.** Very young mothers and mothers over 35 may need additional support
- **Where she works.** Your midwife will want to determine whether your CO's job may pose a risk to her pregnancy
- **Her lifestyle.** The main concern will be if you or your CO smokes and if your CO drinks alcohol. Both of these can affect your BT's health and development. You and your CO are in this together. If you're not already, you both need to adopt a healthy lifestyle: eating well, no drinking and no smoking. Getting fit or maintaining fitness levels is also good for both of you. See *Chapter 3: Fit for fatherhood* for tips and advice

Your midwife will want to take some important measurements, and give your CO some important tests:
- Your CO will have her **height and weight** measured and her body mass index (BMI) calculated.
    - A high BMI (over 30) may indicate that your CO has a higher risk of developing gestational diabetes and other complications. Your CO may need additional medical support
    - A low BMI (under 18) may indicate that your CO is at risk of giving birth to a BT with a low birthweight. Your CO may need additional medical support
- **Blood samples** will be taken to be tested for:
    - Immunity to rubella (German measles)
    - Iron levels (to see if your CO is anaemic)
    - Her blood group, and whether she is rhesus positive or negative
    - An optional screening for HIV, syphilis and hepatitis B
- An optional screening for Down's syndrome and spina bifida, if they are offered in your local area and if your CO is happy to have them. Screening for Down's syndrome may also involve a nuchal translucency scan (see below for more information)
- **A urine sample** will be taken at this and all subsequent appointments, to check for the following:

- Protein, which can be an indicator of a number of issues including a urine infection, high blood pressure, a kidney disorder or diabetes. From 20 weeks and beyond, protein may also indicate pre-eclampsia, a potentially serious condition characterised by protein in the urine and the onset of high blood pressure
- Blood, which could indicate an infection
- Glucose, which could indicate gestational diabetes (meaning your CO's blood sugar level is too high)
- At this and all subsequent appointments, your CO's blood pressure will be taken. High blood pressure can be an indicator of pre-eclampsia

Your midwife will also want to understand your CO's plans for her pregnancy and childbirth. This includes:

- **Where your CO would like to have your BT.** Your midwife will be able to provide information about all the different options available in your area
- **If you would like to attend antenatal classes.** Your midwife will be able to provide details of available classes in your area. See below for more information about antenatal classes
- **If your CO intends to breastfeed.** It's good to get as much information about breastfeeding as possible, so that you and your CO can make a judgement about whether it will work for your unit. Your midwife will be able to provide you with information about breastfeeding and also whether there are local classes or support groups in your area
- **Maternity benefits.** Your CO has maternity rights and can also claim benefits. Your midwife can show her how

Your midwife will also be able to provide your CO with key information that she needs to know for the journey ahead. This includes:
- **Your BT's development.**
- **How your CO can ensure optimal health during pregnancy.**

This includes lifestyle, diet, vitamins and exercise
- **Antenatal care.** Forthcoming appointments and scans, screening tests, antenatal education, breastfeeding classes

At the end of the appointment, your CO will receive notes that record the results of the tests (with the exception of the blood test, which will need to be sent to a lab for testing) and a plan of care. You will both need to take care of these notes as they will need to be taken to every subsequent appointment.

! EMOTION ALERT

Scans and tests can be stressful. These feelings may be exacerbated if you and your CO have a history of miscarriage or if you are already feeling anxious about the pregnancy. When waiting for medical staff or test results, try to remain calm. Don't anticipate outcomes.

If you do get a result that you may not have expected, don't panic. Ask any questions you need to fully understand the implications. If you and your CO have to make a difficult decision based on a test result, try to remain calm. Remember to listen to each other.

SCAN: Dating scan
Eight to 14 weeks
This first ultrasound scan will provide a more reliable due date for your BT's deployment. It will also confirm whether your CO is expecting a single BT or twins or multiples. It provides an opportunity to screen for possible abnormalities.

This is also an opportunity for both of you to see your BT for the first time. At eight weeks you will be able to discern your BT's head and limb buds, and a heartbeat. At this moment, everything becomes very, very real.

! EMOTION ALERT

Nothing can prepare you for how you will feel when you see your BT for the first time. It was a life-changing moment for me that triggered really powerful emotions that I wasn't expecting. Be prepared.

ADVICE FROM THE FRONT LINE

'I was not prepared for the first scan. I had seen other people's photos before and paid little attention to be honest – including my own sister's BT. But seeing your own little one moving in real time is an unforgettable moment.'

PHIL SOWERBY

TELLING PEOPLE

You may feel after 12 weeks, when the first trimester is over and the risk of miscarriage is reduced, that you want to start to tell people. Your nearest and dearest may already have noticed that your CO is behaving differently and that your lifestyle may have changed – both giving up smoking or drinking for example – and so may suspect. Don't be disappointed if this is the case. They're happy for you both. Enjoy it.

! EMOTION ALERT

It can be quite difficult to tell your own parents that you're going to become a parent yourself. It may bring up all kinds of emotions, depending on the relationship that you have with them. Bear in mind that this is a life-changing moment for them too, as they are going to become grandparents to your BT. If this is the first time that they have become grandparents, it may take a while to sink in.

ADVICE FROM THE FRONT LINE

'I am very matter of fact about these sorts of things, but I was still feeling nervous and proud to be telling my dad. Not for any macho reason of "look Dad, I've got swimmers!" but because it's a real life experience that we can share and brings us closer together.'

PHIL SOWERBY

SCAN: Nuchal translucency scan or triple test (if required)
Eleven to 14 weeks

Both the nuchal translucency scan and triple test are designed to indicate the probability of there being a problem. It will not determine whether your BT will definitely be affected, but will help you both decide whether you wish to have a diagnostic (invasive) test to be certain. See 'Diagnostic tests' (page 40) for more information.

Nuchal translucency scan

Sometimes known as the nuchal fold scan, the nuchal translucency scan, like all scans, is optional. It is a screening test that measures the amount of fluid under the skin at the back of your BT's neck as an indicator of chromosomal abnormalities such as Down's syndrome. Your CO will only have this scan if it is on offer in your area and if she opts to have it. If she does choose to have it, then it is possible for it to be carried out at the same time as the dating scan (as long as the scan is between 11 and 14 weeks). It is advisable that she attends this scan with you or a friend or relative for support.

Triple test

This is an alternative to a nuchal translucency scan that some hospitals offer instead. It is a blood test where levels of three substances in your CO's blood are measured:

- **Alpha-fetoprotein (AFP):** a protein produced by your BT's liver
- **Unconjugated estriol (UE):** a protein produced in your CO's placenta and in your BT's liver
- **Human chorionic gonadotropin (hCG):** a hormone produced by your CO's placenta

The blood needs to be sent away for analysis and results are usually back in seven to ten days. It may be advisable for your CO to pick up the results with you, a friend or relative for support.

Diagnostic tests

Diagnostic tests help determine the chances of your BT being born with a chromosomal disorder. Your CO may be offered these if the nuchal translucency scan indicated the possibility of abnormalities, if either of you has a close family member with a chromosomal condition or if your CO is over 35. Diagnostic tests do carry a slight risk of miscarriage and you will both need to discuss and understand the pros and cons with your midwife before proceeding.

Diagnostic tests are invasive and involve inserting a needle into your CO's uterus (after local anaesthetic has been administered) to extract cells that can be examined and tested for a number of conditions:

- CV or chorionic villus sampling: cells from the placenta – chorionic villi – are removed for testing. This test can be taken between 10 and 13 weeks
- Amniocentesis: cells that your BT has shed are in the amniotic fluid and a sample of this fluid is removed for testing. This test can be taken between 15 and 20 weeks

SECOND APPOINTMENT
Sixteen weeks

- Your CO will be able to review, discuss and record the results of the blood tests taken at the booking appointment and also any screening tests

- Your CO will have her blood pressure measured and her urine tested for protein, blood and glucose
- Your midwife will also be able to answer any questions you both may have about the next scan – the anomaly scan
- Your midwife may be able to pick up your BT's heartbeat from around 16 weeks, using a hand-held Doppler (a fetal monitor) that amplifies the sound so that you and your CO will also be able to hear it. Less often, a midwife may have a Pinard stethoscope (an ear trumpet). Be aware that your BT's heartbeat will be racing: their heart typically beats between 120 and 160 beats per minute, compared to our 60 to 100

TOP TIP COMMANDO DAD TOP TIP

There is a huge difference between not being able to hear a fetal heartbeat and a fetal heartbeat not being present. Although it is obviously very reassuring for you and your CO to be able to hear your BT's heartbeat, sometimes, depending on a number of factors, it may not be possible. These include the size of your BT, their position, the position of the placenta and the position of your CO's uterus.

SCAN: Anomaly scan
Eighteen to 22 weeks

This scan will confirm whether your BT is developing normally. This is also the scan where you can find out the sex of your BT, should you choose to. Let the sonographer know either way beforehand.

This scan is also another trigger to tell people who may not already know about your BT, and also to begin to buy the things they'll need. For tips on what to buy, see *Chapter 5: Report to the stores.*

! **EMOTION ALERT**

This is a milestone and you may feel relief and confidence that everything is progressing as it should. It could also be the point where you hear that there may be an issue. In this instance, ask any questions you need to fully understand the implications. If you and your CO need to progress to further tests, try to remain calm. Do not anticipate outcomes. Accept the help and support that is offered.

THIRD APPOINTMENT
Twenty-five weeks
- Your CO will have her blood pressure measured and her urine tested for protein, blood and glucose
- The midwife will:
  - Measure your CO's uterus to check everything is developing normally
  - Give her an abdominal examination – a palpation – by moving her hands over your CO's abdomen
  - Possibly listen to your BT's heartbeat

FOURTH TO SIXTH APPOINTMENTS
Every three weeks between 28 and 34 weeks
- Your CO will have her blood pressure measured and her urine tested for protein, and perhaps blood and glucose (blood and glucose testing is optional)
- The midwife will:
  - Measure your CO's uterus to check everything is developing normally
  - Give her an abdominal examination
  - Possibly listen to your BT's heartbeat
- If your CO's blood is rhesus negative she will be offered anti-D treatments. This is an injection that will prevent her body producing antibodies against their rhesus positive foetus. The first treatment will be offered at 28 weeks and then again at 34 weeks

SEVENTH APPOINTMENT
Thirty-six weeks

- Your CO will have her blood pressure measured and her urine tested for protein, and perhaps blood and glucose
- The midwife will:
  - Measure your CO's uterus to check everything is developing normally
  - Give her an abdominal examination and check the position of your BT
  - Possibly listen to your BT's heartbeat
- Your midwife will also want to give your CO information about:
  - Feeding and caring for your new BT
  - Vitamin K – an optional injection given to your BT after birth to prevent spontaneous bleeding – and screening tests for your newborn baby
  - Your CO's health after your BT is deployed
  - Baby blues – what it is and how your CO can deal with it
  - Postnatal depression – how to recognise and deal with it

TOP TIP

COMMANDO DAD TOP TIP

There is no such thing as a stupid question. This is your first BT, whereas the professionals have taken an active part in many, many births. If you think of a question when you're not in an appointment, jot it down or make a note on your phone and keep it close.

ADVICE FROM THE FRONT LINE

'Go to every appointment you can. Simple. Your CO is going through a lot of emotions and changes. I had a Post-it note full of questions when I went to the appointments. Your CO will be more concerned with the immediate issues as she should and may not remember

everything she wanted to ask. Read all the literature you can, you may relate to some of it, may believe or trust none of it, but some of it will stick. The literature is not there to scare you.'
JAMES FENWICK

EIGHTH AND NINTH APPOINTMENTS
Thirty-eight and forty weeks
- Your CO will have her blood pressure measured and her urine tested for protein, and perhaps blood and glucose
- The midwife will:
  - Measure your CO's uterus to check everything is developing normally
  - Give her an abdominal examination and check the position of your BT
  - Possibly listen to your BT's heartbeat
- At the 40 weeks appointment, your CO will be given more information about what happens if her pregnancy lasts longer than 41 weeks

TENTH APPOINTMENT
Forty-one weeks
- Your CO will have her blood pressure measured and her urine tested for protein, and perhaps blood and glucose
- The midwife will:
  - Measure your CO's uterus to check everything is developing normally
  - Give her an abdominal examination and check the position of your BT
  - Possibly listen to your BT's heartbeat
- As your BT still hasn't deployed, your CO may be offered an

'induction', where her labour is started artificially. See 'Induction' in *Chapter 6: Deployment day* for more information about different methods of induction

3D AND 4D SCANS

In addition to the scans above, you may wish to have a 3D or 4D scan (the fourth dimension being time, meaning you can see your BT moving in real time on the screen). This will need to be arranged, and paid for, privately.

If you do choose to have this type of scan, the best time is between 26 and 30 weeks. This is because your BT will have a layer of fat (so they'll look like you'd expect a newborn to) but their head won't have gone deep into your CO's pelvis. Be aware that you may not be able to get a view or a picture of your BT's face – this will depend on their position.

THE BIRTH PLAN

You and your CO may want to write a birth plan. This will outline how you both would ideally like the labour and birth to go, including pain relief and where and how your CO would like to give birth. You will also be able to discuss what your role should be during labour. You may decide together with your CO that you don't attend the birth. As only one person is usually allowed in the delivery room with your CO, she may choose to have a relative or friend with her, for part or all of the labour. Whatever works for your own family unit is the right way. Don't let anyone else judge the decisions you take.

It's important to be aware that your birth plan is just that – a plan – and that like all plans, it may need to change to keep pace with fast-moving events. On the big day, certain facilities may not be available, or there may be complications, or your CO may simply change her mind. If the latter is the case, ensure that your CO does not waste any energy on disappointment or, worse, guilt. Labour is a marathon, not a sprint. Anything your CO needs along the way should be given to her. And quickly.

ANTENATAL CLASSES

Antenatal classes are designed to provide your CO and you with more information about pregnancy, labour, looking after a newborn BT and what help and support is available to you. They also give you and your CO an opportunity to meet other local parents-to-be in an informal setting.

Although called a class, they're not there to teach you and your CO the perfect way to deliver and look after your BT. There isn't a perfect way. Rather, it's an interactive experience where you get the benefit of an expert sharing information with you, and you get to ask lots of questions. Remain open-minded and gather as much information about the options available to you as possible, so that you can make informed choices.

Antenatal classes are not mandatory, and it is up to you and your CO to find out what's available and to book yourselves on to a course that best suits you. They fill very quickly and it is advisable to book early. You or your CO should ask about antenatal classes available in your local area in one of your earliest appointments and also check out websites that include local listings for antenatal classes.

You can attend as many different classes as you want to, but be aware that there are fees associated with some. You might want to supplement your antenatal classes with specialist workshops dedicated to topics such as breastfeeding, multiple births, water birth or home birth, for example.

ADVICE FROM THE FRONT LINE

'I was pretty clueless about the whole thing and learned A LOT going to the antenatal classes. It was a great place to meet other prospective dads who were in the same frame of mind as me i.e. freaking out a little bit.'
NEIL WHITE

Timing

If your CO is having a single BT, she ideally needs to have antenatal classes from her third trimester (from 27 weeks onwards) and have them completed by week 39. If your CO is carrying more than one BT, she is likely to deliver early and so will need to complete antenatal classes sooner: 34 weeks for twins and 30 weeks for multiple births. For more information on antenatal care for COs carrying more than one BT, see the 'Multiple deployments' section in *Chapter 9: Special ops.*

Be aware that, as with antenatal appointments, you do not have the right to take time off work to attend antenatal classes. However, your wife legally can take time off work if a doctor or midwife has recommended that she attend.

Types of classes

There are two types available, NHS and private.

NHS

These antenatal classes are free and typically take place at the hospital where your CO will give birth or nearby children's centres. The midwives will have the inside track on the local maternity services and the policies and procedures of the hospital where your CO is giving birth. You may be given the opportunity to see the maternity unit.

There will be regional differences though, so check – early – what is available in your area.

Private antenatal classes

You may need to pay for these. Numbers may be restricted. These include:

- National Childbirth Trust (NCT) classes
- Classes offered by local providers
- Online antenatal classes

The National Childbirth Trust (NCT)

The NCT runs antenatal classes throughout the United Kingdom. These classes are typically smaller than NHS ones and venues can vary. The teachers are all university-accredited antenatal teachers who have to meet standards in order to get their annual license to practice. They will be familiar with the local maternity services and be able to provide information about the available facilities. There will be a fee, which varies by area, but there are concessions available. If you are interested in attending an NCT antenatal class, ring your local provider for more information. See page 155 for contact details.

Classes offered by other local providers

Do some research to find out what's available in your local area (see 'How do I find out what's available?' page 51). Fees will vary. Local providers may give antenatal classes and also specialist classes that you may find a useful supplement.

 ADVICE FROM THE FRONT LINE

'It's a good idea to attend antenatal classes from a social and support side of things. I don't come from, or work in, the place that we now live in and had our son.

So the social group for me and Katherine was pretty small. Having a group of people all thinking the same things, asking the same questions and able to express concern and support for each other through pregnancy and the first year (so far) has been invaluable. We still hook up for play dates and we've had a couple of dads' nights out too, which has helped us stay in touch with the rest of the world!'

NICK DAWSON

Online

Online classes are increasingly available and getting more sophisticated. It's possible to watch high-quality video (and rewatch it later) and possibly chat online to other parents-to-be and midwives. They're not local and so you and your CO will need to speak to your midwife or doctor about local maternity facilities, but they will cover the main topics. Securing a place on them shouldn't be a problem and it removes the issue of whether you can attend all of the classes. Some providers do charge a fee.

Finding the right antenatal class

What antenatal class you and your CO sign up for will depend on what you want to get out of them. Here are some things to bear in mind:

- Most classes will cover the main topics, although some may focus on certain aspects more than others:
  - Health and wellbeing of your CO and BT
  - Labour and childbirth
  - Advice on breathing and relaxation techniques
  - Pain relief options
  - Early parenthood: physical changes and looking after a newborn

BT, including breastfeeding
- You may wish to find an antenatal class that supports your circumstances, for example:
  - Twins or multiples
  - Very young mothers
- You may wish to find an antenatal class that supports the decisions you and your CO have made around labour and childbirth. Or you may wish to sign up for specialist classes or workshops to supplement your antenatal classes. For example:
  - Active birth: where your CO stays active during labour to achieve a natural birth
  - Home birth
  - Water birth
  - Natural (i.e. drug-free) birth
  - Caesarean birth
  - HypnoBirthing: where your CO uses self-hypnosis during labour and childbirth
- Exercise all the usual caution if booking an independent course and check the experience and qualifications of the course provider

ADVICE FROM THE FRONT LINE

'The antenatal classes provided more than information – they provided friendships. People like you, going though the same fears, apprehensions and questions.'
MARK BAKER

Men-only antenatal classes

There may be men-only antenatal classes available in your area or within what you consider to be a reasonable travelling distance.

The Fatherhood Institute provide a training programme for expectant dads called *Hit the Ground Crawling*. It is available throughout the UK and is facilitated by trained midwives, health visitors or children's centre staff. It not only provides the information that you would expect to be covered in an antenatal class, but will also provide you with the opportunity to learn childcare skills directly from new dads and their BTs.

ADVICE FROM THE FRONT LINE

'Having a BT on the way is an amazing experience and you should embrace it.'

JAMES FENWICK

How do I find out what's available?

You can find out about antenatal classes in your area in the following places:

- Your midwife or doctor
- Other parents-to-be or new parents
- National Childbirth Trust: www.nct.org.uk
- Noticeboards in your doctor's surgery
- Local papers
- Websites that include local listings:
  - Netmums: www.netmums.com
  - Mumsnet (find your local Mumsnet via the site: www.mumsnet.com)
- Websites that provide online antenatal classes:
  - Baby Centre: www.babycentre.co.uk
  - Antenatal Online: www.antenatalonline.co.uk
  - Netmums: www.netmums.com

PATERNITY LEAVE AND PAY

Paternity leave is time that you can take off from work to support your CO. There are two types:

- Ordinary Paternity Leave (one or two weeks, taken consecutively)
- Additional Paternity Leave (up to an extra twenty-six weeks' leave, taken consecutively)

Ordinary Paternity Leave cannot start before your BT is deployed, but must be completed within the eight weeks afterwards. To qualify for Ordinary Paternity Leave, you will need to be an employee and have worked for your employer for twenty-six weeks, ending with the fifteenth week before your BT is due, and continue to be employed until your BT is deployed. In other words, you need to have worked for your employer for at least as long as your CO has been pregnant. Ordinary Statutory Paternity Pay is the legal minimum your employer must pay you while you're on Ordinary Paternity Leave.

You don't qualify for paternity leave unless you have a contract of employment (which rules out the self-employed and may affect some agency workers and contractors. If you don't qualify for paternity leave with your employer, you are still entitled under law to take unpaid emergency leave to be with your CO as she goes through labour. Of course, you can also choose to use your annual leave or to take unpaid leave.

If your CO returns to work before the end of her maternity leave, you may have the right to take up to twenty-six weeks' leave, called Additional Paternity Leave. This additional leave can only start once your BT is at least twenty weeks old and must be finished by their first birthday.

Additional Paternity Pay is available, but will end when your CO's maternity pay would have ended. If you are eligible for Additional Paternity Leave but not pay, you may take this additional leave unpaid.

Letting your employer know

If you intend to take paternity leave, you must notify your employer at least fifteen weeks before your BT is due. Your application for Ordinary Statutory Paternity Pay needs to be submitted at least four weeks before you wish to start receiving it. The easiest way is to do both of these things at once and download form SC3 'Becoming a parent' from the HM Revenue & Customs website and submit it to your employer.

Sometimes there are valid reasons for not providing fifteen weeks' notice: for example, if your BT is premature or your CO's pregnancy is discovered very late. In these instances, simply give as much notice as possible. Forgetting to submit paperwork is not a valid reason.

Once your BT has deployed, you'll need to tell your employer as soon as you practically can.

These are the minimum terms for paternity leave. Your employer may offer better terms, so speak to your HR department in the first instance for guidance and advice.

For more information on statutory paternity leave and pay, including eligibility details, Additional Paternity Leave and statutory weekly rates of pay, please see the Gov UK website: www.gov.uk/paternity-pay-leave.

RECAP AND REFRESH

Chapter 2: Actions on appointments has provided:

- A review of scans and appointments your CO will need to attend. The list of tests, scans and check-ups presented in the chapter might seem daunting, but they will soon become routine for you and your CO
- Information about antenatal classes and how to book them. Book them early
- Paternity leave and pay
- You may wish to start buying things for your BT after the first trimester has ended, or your CO has had the anomaly scan. For

advice on what to buy, go to *Chapter 5: Report to the stores*
- If you and your CO are expecting twins or multiples, you can find additional information about antenatal scans and appointments in the 'Multiple deployments' section of *Chapter 9: Special ops*
- *Chapter 10: Breaking the code* provides definitions for some medical terms that you may come across in your CO's notes. If you have any concerns, speak to your midwife or your CO's doctor

Fit for fatherhood

3

THE BRIEF

Few occasions in life will present you with an opportunity to take stock of your life more than finding out you're going to be a dad. Grab it with both hands. Take a long hard look at your levels of health and fitness and your lifestyle. This is not only to enable you to be fit for the impending rigours of early fatherhood – but also for the many years of fathering adventures that lie ahead.

THE OBJECTIVE

By the end of this chapter you will know about changes you can easily make to your lifestyle, fitness levels and eating habits that will help you to be fit for fatherhood. If you're already a perfect physical specimen, your challenge will be to maintain that: the early stages of fatherhood are a prime time to put on weight due to poor diet and physical inactivity. See page 62 for tips on fitting in exercise around family commitments.

ADVICE FROM THE FRONT LINE

'Something I tell other would-be fathers is that they need to look after themselves. Nutrition and exercise are important as well as getting as much sleep as possible. I kept exercising before and after.'

NEIL WHITE

LIFESTYLE

SMOKING

If you smoke, stop. There's never going to be a better incentive. Cigarette smoke, either from your CO smoking directly or by her breathing in your cigarette smoke, restricts the essential oxygen supply to your developing BT. This can cause a whole host of problems, which you can prevent. I can't tell you that giving up cigarettes will be easy, but I can assure you that it will be easier to live with than causing harm to your unborn BT.

There is a lot of help and support available to help conquer your physical addiction and your psychological habit. 'Smokefree' is an NHS website that can help you stop smoking. It features information about the different methods of quitting, motivational activities, a free helpline and online chat functionality. It also has a section on 'Fathers and smoking': www.smokefree.nhs.uk.

If your CO smokes, she needs to stop too. There's an NHS Pregnancy Smoking Helpline on 0800 169 9 169 that she can ring to be put in touch with professionals who will provide her with non-judgemental advice about the best way to stop. She can ring at any time. Her midwife and doctor will also be able to support her.

How can I practically help my CO to give up smoking?

- Support and encourage her. The more stressed she is, the more likely she is to feel she needs a cigarette
- If you're smoking, stop
- Remove physical traces of smoking from your home and car: cigarettes, ashtrays, lighters etc
- Avoid social situations where people may be smoking and replace them with ones where smoking is less likely
- Tell family and friends and ask them to be supportive

DRINKING

Now is a good time to review your drinking habits. Even if you are a light or moderate drinker, you'll be pleasantly surprised by the effect that cutting back or removing alcohol will have on your sleep (it will improve immediately), your energy levels and perhaps even your weight. But cutting down drinking has long-term benefits too – reducing your risk of health issues such as high blood pressure, heart disease, cancer and liver cirrhosis.

As backup support to your CO, you're also going to want to support her as she cuts out alcohol altogether or reduces consumption to the lowest levels.

ADVICE FROM THE FRONT LINE

'I cut right down on my drinking before and certainly after my BT was born. I wanted to be clear-headed and to be able to support my wife in the lead-up to the birth – especially nearer the due date. And once the wee fellow was born, I didn't drink for the first few weeks as sleep was at a premium and we didn't know when we would be woken up. The last thing I wanted

was to be fuzzy-headed in the middle of the night when my mind had to be on the little BT.'
CALUM BEATT

If your CO drinks alcohol when pregnant, it crosses the placenta into the bloodstream of your unborn BT. The National Institute for Health and Care Excellence (NICE) advises that alcohol should be avoided completely during the first three months of pregnancy as it may increase the risk of miscarriage. Beyond that period, low levels of alcohol – one or two units twice a week – are recommended. This is not a guarantee that there will be no adverse effect on your BT. The only way to guarantee there are no ill effects is for your CO not to drink at all.

Excessive drinking can have devastating effects on your unborn BT. Fetal Alcohol Syndrome (FAS) can cause facial deformities and problems with physical and emotional development.

The charity Drinkaware has a website with practical tips, inspiration and straightforward advice on steps you can take to reduce your alcohol consumption. It also has a section on 'Alcohol and pregnancy': www.drinkaware.co.uk.

If your CO thinks she may benefit from support to help her stop drinking, she can speak to her midwife or doctor.

What is one unit?

A unit is a measure of alcohol, but most drinks are usually over one unit. Some examples:

- Small (25 ml) measure of spirits (vodka, gin, rum, whisky etc): 1 unit
- Small (125 ml) glass of wine: 1.5 units
- Half a pint of lager: 1.5 units
- A bottle of beer: 1.7 units

Drinkaware has an alcohol unit calculator on their site.

How can I practically help my CO to stop – or reduce – drinking?
- Support and encourage her
- Cut down the amount that you drink or stop altogether
- Avoid social situations where people may be drinking and replace them with ones where drinking is less likely
- Tell family and friends and ask them to be supportive

FITNESS

Fatherhood requires strength and stamina and there's never a better time to adopt a healthier lifestyle and improve your fitness than right now. This will not only deliver the obvious health benefits, but also help you better deal with the hectic lifestyle of a new dad.

ADVICE FROM THE FRONT LINE

'I'm not a particularly fit guy, but I took the opportunity to get fit before the arrival of our BT by signing up for the Great North Run. I found that with increased fitness levels I am able to cope better with less sleep, manage stress considerably better, effectively keep base camp in order and provide support to my wife.'
STEVE COOPER

The most important thing you need when getting – and staying – fit is the right mindset. It's this that will get you going in the early days and keep you going as you incorporate long-term changes into your lifestyle. Being fit isn't just about achieving a certain goal (although goals can be great motivators), it's about habitually making better choices when it comes to diet, exercise and lifestyle. Don't be put off by this. Good habits may be hard to form, but they're easy to live with. Keep at it.

If you need some ideas about how you can get fit, take a look at the Health and Fitness pages on the NHS Choices website. It is packed with tips – including getting fit for free – guidelines, advice and fitness plans: www.nhs.uk/Livewell/fitness/

ADVICE FROM THE FRONT LINE

'This was a major part of the pregnancy for me – I was determined to be in the best shape of my life for when baby arrived. However, I ensured that my routine was tailored to the wife so that it didn't interfere with me being able to look after and support her.' PAUL HOPE

Maintaining fitness

When your trooper deploys, you will need to master the art of fitting in exercise around your family commitments. Time is going to be in short supply, especially in the first few months when your BT is getting into a schedule.

ADVICE FROM THE FRONT LINE

'I've always played football/boxed/Ju Jitsu. I fully believe in healthy body, healthy mind. I believe it will help me cope with my child's demands and keep me fit and healthy as they grow up. I want to be active with them and maybe coach the football team in later years (of course, they may not like football!)'

GRANT MILLS

- **Go out and about with your BT.** In the early days, this could be just getting out for a walk in the fresh air with your BT and CO. Sorties can become more adventurous as time passes: you can go hiking, jogging and cycling with your BT. Try to increase the intensity during your shorter missions. There is lots of evidence that vigorous intensity exercise is much better for maintaining and increasing fitness than slow plodding exercise. You should just be able to hold a conversation during your fast walks

ADVICE FROM THE FRONT LINE

'I've been going swimming with my BT as soon as she had had her first jabs; the confidence she now has even at 13 weeks is amazing. It also gives me real one-on-one

> *quality time with her, which is the best thing ever. It also makes bath time far more fun!'*
> ANDY LONG
>
> *'My plan is to get a cycle trailer to take my BT out on the bike as soon as she is old enough.'*
> KEVIN S

- **If you're at work, try to fit exercise into your schedule:**
  - Getting to work:
    - Cycle to work if possible. If you don't have a bike, look into 'Cyclescheme' (www.cyclescheme.co.uk) – it may help you get a bike tax-free (saving about 40%) and paid monthly out of your pay
    - If commuting, get off the bus or train one stop earlier and walk the difference. Park the car further away from the office and walk in
  - At work, keep physically active. Take the stairs, walk to your colleagues' desks rather than phoning them and stand as much as possible. Standing doubles the amount of energy that your body uses
  - If you can get an hour at lunch, see if there is a local gym that you can use or get out and go for a walk or a jog
- **If you're at home:**
  - Become more efficient at exercising. Create – or find – a fifteen minute routine that allows you to give yourself a total body workout. Fifteen minutes is the optimum amount of time because even a very young BT will nap for fifteen minutes
  - Do exercise that requires little – or no – kit: sit-ups, press-ups, skipping and squats are all fabulous exercises that you can

perform in confined spaces at a moment's notice. And that may be all you have. Adopt an exercise lifestyle routine in the same way you will be adopting new routines with your BT

- Get exercise kit you can use at home and be disciplined enough to use it

- **If you are training for an event.** Ideally, you're going to need the full support of your CO, not only for their help in looking after your BT while you train, but also as a motivating force to help you to stick to your schedule. This can be tricky if you need to train at times that you previously spent with your partner (especially if you are training for an event and your training time is increasing). If this is an issue for you, tackle it now. It is not going to go away. Here's how I did it:
  - I explained to my CO why I really wanted to train and compete
  - I worked to ensure she had as much 'free' time as I had training time. This is especially important as your CO is going to need time away from your BT. Looking after a newborn BT is a physically and emotionally demanding job
  - I stuck it out and proved I was serious

If you do need to train away from base camp, avoid busy times in the family day: i.e. mealtimes, bedtime etc, as all hands need to be on deck then. If you are working, be aware that your CO may be looking forward to you getting home so that she can have a break from looking after your BT, and also spend time with you. Either get up early and create time at the start of the day (I prefer this) or be prepared to go out in the evening when your BT is asleep. Although sometimes you may find it hard to get out to train, you will feel so much better afterwards.

Maintaining or improving your fitness is essential for your own wellbeing as well as for those around you. Maintaining a range of endurance and strength will help you in the future with your BT, whether lifting them around the house or playing in the park.

NUTRITION

A good diet is a long-term investment in your future. It will keep you healthy and well now, delivering many benefits such as more energy, better sleep and increased concentration. But it will also reduce your risk of developing illness (e.g. cancer, heart disease etc) later on. For your CO, a good diet is obviously essential as she needs to keep herself

healthy not only to cope with the rigours of pregnancy and motherhood, but also to help your BT develop and grow.

ADVICE FROM THE FRONT LINE

'A good diet is essential for keeping your energy levels up. In the final weeks preceding deployment, do some cooking of meals you can freeze.'

JOHN ALLEN

Eating for two

Your CO may feel hungrier than normal because of the demands on her body, but 'eating for two' is a myth. On average, a CO will only need to eat about 300 calories more (although your midwife can advise your CO based on her personal circumstances). Quantity isn't really the issue so much as quality. The good news is that you can both share the same healthy diet, and ensure that you, your CO and BT all have the nourishment you need.

TOP TIP

COMMANDO DAD TOP TIP

In the early weeks, your CO's eating habits may go awry as her body gets used to soaring hormones and a heightened sense of taste and smell causes food aversions and cravings. You may be concerned if she is craving unhealthy foods, full of saturated fat and sugar. You're right to be concerned as your CO and BT need a balanced diet in order to thrive, but tread carefully. Your CO is going through a huge period of change and she does not need to be lectured on a healthy diet. What she does need is support from you to indulge her unhealthy cravings a little, and her healthy cravings a lot.

Try to find alternatives where possible. For example, my wife craved spinach and tomatoes, but she wanted them on a pizza, two or three times a day. Through trial and error we found that wilted spinach and garlic, and a glass of tomato juice with Worcestershire sauce, curbed the cravings for pizza. It also helped that I followed a healthy diet too. She knew she had my support 100% and that if our diet was good for us, it was going to be good for our BT.

If your CO is only making unhealthy food choices, especially beyond those first few weeks, then encourage her to speak to her midwife or doctor for advice. If she has cravings for non-food items (a condition called 'pica') then she should not indulge these without first seeking medical advice as they are potentially harmful to her and your BT.

ADVICE FROM THE FRONT LINE

'I wish I had known the dietary needs for mother and child – my partner developed gestational diabetes, which could have been avoided through diet.' RON MURRAY

Food groups

Nutritionists advise that the recommended daily intake of certain types of foods is as follows:

Food group	Purpose	Types of food	Amount
Grains Cereals Milk and dairy Potatoes	Energy Fibre Vitamins Minerals	• All breads: white, brown, granary, wholemeal, soda bread etc • Rice • Grains e.g. wheat, corn, barley, buckwheat, millet, oats etc • Pasta, noodles, couscous • Potatoes	• These should form the main part of your meal • Include at least one food from this group at every meal • Wholegrain is the best
Fruits and vegetables	Fibre, vitamins minerals Source of antioxidants	• All fruit and vegetables: fresh and frozen • Fruit and vegetable juices • Peas, beans and sweetcorn	• Eat at least five portions of fruit and vegetables a day, prioritising vegetables over fruit as they have the same health benefits but less sugar
Milk and dairy	Calcium Protein Vitamins Minerals	• Milk • Cheese • Yogurt • Fromage frais	• Eat three portions a day • Choose low-fat dairy products. They have the same amount of calcium
Meat, fish and non-dairy protein	Protein Vitamins Minerals Fibre (pulses)	• Meat: beef, pork, lamb • Fish: fresh, frozen and tinned • Eggs • Poultry: chicken and turkey • Pulses: beans, peas, lentils • Nuts • Soy protein	• Include foods from this category every day • Aim to include at least two portions of fish per week, especially oily • Choose lean cuts of meat, remove any visible fat from the meat or the skin from poultry
Fats	Energy Vitamins	• Butter, margarine, low-fat spread, cooking oils, lard etc • Mayonnaise, salad cream, oily dressings • Cream	• Limit this group

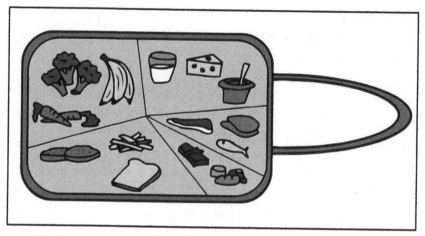

Portion plate containing all the food groups you, your CO and BT need.

Processed foods

If something has been done to your food before it gets to your plate, it has been processed. Try to avoid processed food if possible. If you eat food in its natural state, your body can recognise it and use it efficiently. The more processed your food is, the more likely it is to contain high levels of sugar, salt and saturated fat. They are typically high in calories.

There are obvious processed foods that we all know to avoid: biscuits, cakes, fizzy drinks, chocolate, sweets, crisps and pastries. However, there are foods that we may not necessarily think of as 'processed' that we should also limit. These include:
- White pasta, rice and breads. Eat wholegrain
- Fruit and vegetable juices. The fibre has been removed
- Breakfast cereals. Check sugar and salt levels

Foods your CO should avoid

There are certain foods that your CO should avoid during pregnancy, as they are thought to increase the chance of getting listeriosis (where the food is contaminated by bacteria called listeria). These include:

- Soft cheeses (Brie, Camembert, blue cheese, soft goat's cheese etc)
- Unpasteurised milk
- Raw or undercooked eggs (home-made mayonnaise contains raw egg, for example); all eggs must be cooked all the way through, with no runny yolks and a solid white
- Raw or undercooked meat (every piece of meat must be cooked thoroughly, no 'pink' meat)
- Pâté (even vegetarian varieties)

Your CO is at an increased risk of developing listeriosis because her body's defences are weaker and therefore less able to resist the listeria bacteria. Exercise caution. Some countries also advise that pregnant women avoid the following foods, but here in the UK the risk is deemed to be so low that this advice is not given. The choice is yours:

- Cooked, sliced 'deli' meats
- Raw, smoked fish, including smoked salmon

MEDIC: STAND BY

Call your medical support team if your CO has eaten any of the foods above, or inadequately reheated chilled food, and shows early symptoms of listeria infection. These are flu-like symptoms: fever, headache, tiredness, aches and pains.

Other High-Risk Foods

Some foods can contain harmful bacteria and viruses that can cause food poisoning. This will not harm your BT, but will make life miserable for your CO as symptoms include vomiting and diarrhoea. She will already be avoiding some foods that can cause food poisoning, including raw or undercooked meat, raw eggs, soft cheese, pâté and unpasteurised milk. Other foods include:

- Raw shellfish (including mussels, lobster, crab, prawns, scallops and clams). Cold, precooked prawns can be eaten
- Pre-packed sandwiches

Too much vitamin A could potentially harm your BT. Your CO needs to avoid fish liver oil supplements or any supplements containing vitamin A (see page 71 for supplements that your CO can take during pregnancy). Foods rich in vitamin A include:
- Liver
- Liver products such as liver pâté or liver sausage

Certain types of fish contain high levels of mercury, which may damage your BT's developing nervous system and should be avoided completely. These include:
- Shark
- Marlin
- Swordfish

Other types of fish containing mercury can be eaten, but in limited amounts. These include:
- Tuna
  - no more than two tuna steaks a week
  - Four medium-sized tins of tuna a week
- Oily fish (salmon, mackerel, sardines and trout)
  - No more than two portions a week

COMMANDO DAD GOLDEN RULES FOR FOOD PREPARATION
- In addition to limiting or avoiding certain foods, you also need to take care when storing or preparing food. Ensure that your CO's food is cooked until steaming hot throughout. This is especially true if she is eating reheated food or ready meals
- Keep your fridge temperature below 5°C. She does not eat any food that has been out of the fridge for more than 4 hours
- She does not eat any food past its 'use by' date (not the same as 'sell by' or 'display until' dates)
- All raw fruit and vegetables are washed thoroughly before use

Supplements

Even with a diet rich in vitamins and minerals, your CO may need to take pregnancy supplements to ensure she gets the following nutrients. She can check amounts with her midwife or doctor:

- Vitamin D every day throughout pregnancy and breastfeeding
- Folic acid every day, taken until she is at least 12 weeks pregnant
- Iron
- Vitamin C, which amongst other benefits will help your CO's body absorb iron
- Calcium

Pregnancy supplements are available from a number of sources and your CO can ask your midwife for more information. Your CO will need to make sure that she doesn't take a tablet including vitamin A (or retinol) as high levels could harm your BT. Some families may be able to receive free vitamins through the NHS Healthy Start scheme: www. healthystart.nhs.uk.

AN ARMY MARCHES ON ITS STOMACH

We all know that home-cooked food is best, but it's hard to get motivated to start cooking from scratch when it's the end of a long day and you're already hungry. While a takeaway might be a nice treat once in a while, it's not a healthy – or cheap – option, so don't put yourself in that situation. Get organised in advance:

- **When you do have time to cook, make extra portions and freeze them.** This is good practice now and when your BT deploys. You'll be able to take your evening meal out of the freezer in the morning and pop it in a bowl in the fridge to defrost – basically, your own 'ready meal', but one where you know all of the ingredients that went into it.

  My favourites for this are curries, chillies and stews as the flavour actually seems to improve once they have been defrosted and reheated. When you freeze them, remember to label them clearly as freezing is the great leveller: it makes everything look the same. When you're reheating these meals, remember to ensure they are steaming hot, and do not refreeze.

- **Use frozen vegetables.** They will save you time and energy prepping accompaniments to your meal.
- **Master the art of the slow cooker.** The fifteen minutes spent prepping vegetables and sealing meat in the morning could be rewarded with a rich stew that evening. Make extra portions and freeze.
- **Use what you have.** I will often search the internet for inspiration for a meal, based on what I've got in my fridge and freezer. This is great because it not only introduces variety into your cooking, but also saves you money on wasted food.
- **Learn to make your own 'fast food'.** The ultimate fast foods are pasta and noodles. You can make a pasta sauce with about five minutes' prep and a stir-fry will take you three minutes' longer than it takes to chop the vegetables. For optimum nutrition, use wholegrain pasta, noodles and rice.

Search online for your favourite fast foods to see how easy it would be to make them at home from fresh. You'll be surprised how easy it is – I guarantee it. See the Resources section on www.commandodad.com for some of my favourite recipes, including pasta sauce, burgers, fajitas and crispy chicken pieces with healthy chips.

 ADVICE FROM THE FRONT LINE

'I have a simple approach to nutrition. My wife is breastfeeding our BT, I am feeding my wife = what I feed my wife is passed to my baby. We have strictly had vegetables every day, in one form or another. I prepare the evening meal in the morning, which means less to do later in the day when we are both tired.' STEVE COOPER

RECAP AND REFRESH

You need to get fit and healthy to cope with the rigours of fatherhood. If you know you could make improvements, make them now. *Chapter 3: Fit for fatherhood* has provided:

- Tips for giving up smoking and drinking for both you and your CO
- Tips for improving your fitness. Your CO will benefit from exercise too and should keep up her normal daily physical activity as long as she feels comfortable. Her midwife or doctor can answer any questions she might have about exercise, including exercise that she needs to avoid
- Nutrition, including golden rules for preparing food for your CO and foods she needs to limit or avoid
- Basic healthy recipes

RECAP AND REFRESH

Call the medic

4

THE BRIEF
Your CO's body has a huge period of change ahead of it. You need to know how to distinguish between a 'normal' pregnancy ailment and something more serious that may require urgent medical attention. The information below is intended for information only – if you or your CO has any concerns, she should raise these directly with her midwife or doctor.

THE OBJECTIVE
By the end of this chapter you will have an understanding of what's normal – and what isn't – during pregnancy. You'll know how to spot potentially serious physical problems, both physical (e.g. pre-eclampsia) and mental (e.g. antenatal depression).

ADVICE FROM THE FRONT LINE

'Don't be afraid if something doesn't feel right to pick up the phone and speak to the hospital. Everyone we came in contact with was great.'

DAN SAXTON

SYMPTOMS NOT TO IGNORE

Throughout pregnancy, your CO will have a number of symptoms that, while they may be uncomfortable – even painful – frustrating, distressing and sometimes even alarming, are nevertheless considered 'normal'.

However, there are a set of symptoms that must not be ignored as they may indicate a medical problem. These are listed below. Confusingly, some of these will occur during a normal pregnancy – for example, morning sickness, swollen feet and ankles and headaches – and be harmless. However, if these symptoms are persistent and severe, or accompanied by other symptoms, they could indicate a problem. All of the conditions I mention below are explained further in the sections 'Conditions that require urgent medical attention' and 'Pregnancy complications'.

If you are in doubt, pick up the phone to your doctor or midwife.

- **Vaginal bleeding**
  - Light painless spotting may be implantation during early pregnancy and shouldn't cause concern
  - Heavy bleeding with back or abdominal pain needs immediate medical assistance as this may indicate a miscarriage
  - Before 8–10 weeks, if it is accompanied by a severe pain in one side of the lower abdomen it may be a symptom of an ectopic pregnancy

- Sudden bleeding in late pregnancy could be a symptom of placenta praevia, placental abruption or premature labour
- **Leaking fluid**
  - Leaking clear or straw-coloured liquid indicates that your CO's waters could have broken. After 37 weeks this is normal and shouldn't cause concern (although you will need to let your midwife know as your BT is not as protected from infection once her waters are broken)
  - Before 37 weeks she will need to be monitored for infection and possibly prepared for premature labour
- **Abdominal/pelvic pain or pressure:** Lower back pain
  - Before 37 weeks these may be signs of premature labour
- **Increased discharge:** Change in volume of type/volume of discharge
  - After 37 weeks this may be a 'show', a sign your CO's body is preparing for labour, and is normal. The cervix is getting ready to dilate and so the jelly-like mucus plug that has sealed it comes away. It may be tinged brown or pink.
  - Prior to 37 weeks this could be a sign of premature labour
- **Fever or chills**
  This is often an indicator of infection, especially when accompanied by vomiting, and requires treatment
- **Vision problems**
  Blurred vision, double vision, dimming, flashing lights or 'floaters' (spots in her field of vision) for more than two hours could indicate pre-eclampsia
- **Severe headaches**
  Persistent headaches that last more than two or three hours may be a symptom of pre-eclampsia
- Leg cramps
  Leg cramps are a normal part of pregnancy, but may indicate a blood clot in her leg (or deep vein thrombosis) when:
  - It is a persistent or severe leg cramp or calf pain in one leg that

doesn't ease up when she flexes her ankle
- The area is red, swollen and warm to the touch

- **Dizziness**
  Early in pregnancy, severe dizziness, accompanied by vaginal bleeding or severe abdominal pain, could indicate ectopic pregnancy

- **Persistent itching**
  Itching is a normal part of pregnancy as your CO's skin stretches to accommodate her growing body. However, if she gets intense itchiness all over (probably starting in the palms of her hands and the soles of her feet) and she is in the second or third trimester, this may indicate obstetric cholestasis, a liver condition

- **Persistent nausea and/or vomiting**
  These can indicate hyperemesis gravidarum – a debilitating condition, sometimes requiring hospitalisation

- **Swelling**
  Sudden or severe swelling in hands, feet or ankles could indicate pre-eclampsia

- **Urine issues**
  Discomfort, pain, stinging, burning when she pees, or little or no urine could indicate an infection. This will require treatment to prevent it causing more serious problems

- **Depression**
  - While pregnant: unsurprisingly, many women go through mood swings in pregnancy, but if your CO is persistently down, without any positive feelings to balance them out, and she begins to lose interest in work, relationships and even her pregnancy, this may indicate antenatal depression
  - After she has given birth: shortly after birth, your CO may experience the 'baby blues'. However, if this lasts for longer than two weeks and your CO is persistently down or begins to lose interest in the relationship with you or your BT, this may indicate post-natal depression

- **Contractions (prior to 37 weeks)**

  Late in pregnancy, your CO may experience practise contractions called Braxton Hicks. 'Real' contractions differ from these in the following ways:
  - They don't go away. Early contractions may feel like persistent back pain and a crampy, period pain
  - Your CO will be able to feel contractions all over, not just at the front
  - Although they may be irregular to start with, they will get stronger, occur at increasingly shorter intervals, last longer and become more painful
  - The pain will come in a wave, reaching a peak and then tailing off

CONDITIONS THAT REQUIRE URGENT MEDICAL ATTENTION

If your CO displays the symptoms below, call 999 or take her straight to A&E. Do not delay. Do not second guess. A doctor needs to make a diagnosis – and take action – quickly.

Condition	Symptoms to look out for in your CO	Potential problems
Pre-eclampsia Sudden onset of high blood pressure and protein in urine	Over 20 weeks pregnant and experiencing: • Severe headaches • Blurred vision • Severe swelling of hands, feet or ankles • Gaining a lot of weight	In severe cases, a rapid rise in blood pressure can lead to seizure, stroke, multiple organ failure and be fatal to your CO and BT
Placental abruption A condition when the placenta partly or completely separates from the uterus prior to the BT being born	• Vaginal bleeding or spotting • Your CO's waters break and the fluid is bloody • Tenderness or pain in the abdomen • Back pain • Frequent contractions or a single contraction that doesn't stop	Your BT may be born prematurely, have growth problems or, in severe cases, die
Ectopic pregnancy When a fertilised egg implants outside of your CO's uterus, usually in the Fallopian tube	Between 8 and 10 weeks pregnant and experiencing: • Vaginal bleeding • Sudden, sharp and persistent pain in one side of her abdomen • Dizziness • Shoulder tip pain (the place where her shoulder meets her arm) • Diarrhoea and vomiting	There is a serious risk that the Fallopian tube will rupture (burst). In most cases, it can be successfully repaired or removed. In rare cases, a ruptured Fallopian tube can be fatal to your CO
Premature labour Labour before 37 weeks, i.e. before your BT is fully developed	Less than 37 weeks pregnant and experiencing: • Increased vaginal discharge • Pelvic pressure and cramping • Back pain radiating to the abdomen • Contractions	Generally, the later on in the pregnancy your CO is, the better chance your BT has of surviving

PREGNANCY COMPLICATIONS

You will need to draw the following complications to your medical support team's attention:

Condition	Symptoms to look out for in your CO	If not treated
Placenta praevia A condition in which the placenta partially or wholly blocks the neck of the uterus, interfering with the normal delivery of your BT	• Sudden and painless bleeding • Abdominal pain (rare)	Depends how far your CO is into her pregnancy. She may need to go into hospital to be monitored. There is a danger of preterm delivery and your BT may need to be delivered by Caesarean section
Post-natal depression Depression that your CO experiences after your BT is born	• Persistent negative emotions: anxiety, fear, guilt, sadness or hopelessness • Physical manifestations of anxiety: racing heart, sweating, panic attacks • Crying and irritability • Changes in appetite • Taking no pleasure from being with your BT or feeling hostile towards them or you • Exhaustion and lacking in motivation to do anything	Post-natal depression cannot get better without medical intervention
Antenatal depression Depression that your CO experiences before your BT is born	As above, but occurring before your BT is born	Antenatal depression needs to be treated. Some COs go on to develop post-natal depression, but it is not a foregone conclusion
Hyperemesis gravidarum Excessive vomiting	• Severe and persistent nausea or vomiting • Dehydration	Your CO needs fluids and nutrients to nourish her – and your BT. She may need to go to hospital and receive nourishment through an IV drip

Gestational diabetes	Raised blood sugar (your midwife	Can be managed by diet and
Too much sugar in the blood during pregnancy	always checks your BT's urine for glucose). There may also be additional blood tests if needed	possibly insulin injections or Metformin, a tablet. If left untreated it can cause a big baby and an increased risk of premature labour
Obstetric cholestasis	• Severe, persistent itching	Increased concern for your BT's
A build-up of bile acids in the blood producing a persistent itch	• Tiredness • Mild jaundice	wellbeing may mean your CO is induced early, before she is full term

Taking medication

It's not advisable for your CO to take certain medications – even over the counter ones such as paracetamol – during pregnancy as they may cause issues.

If your CO has a condition that means she has to take medication regularly, she will need to speak to her doctor as soon as she knows she is pregnant. They will be able to confirm whether the medicine is safe to take, or suggest alternatives.

Your CO will also need to make sure that medical professionals – her doctor, dentist etc – know that she is pregnant when they are prescribing her any medicines. It is the same for over the counter remedies: she will need to speak to the pharmacist to ensure that the medication she is taking is safe to take during pregnancy.

TOP TIP

COMMANDO DAD TOP TIP

Do not assume that herbal alternatives are safe to take during pregnancy. As with all other medications, you or your CO will need to check with your doctor, midwife or pharmacist.

RECAP AND REFRESH

Chapter 4: Call the medic has provided an overview of 'normal' pregnancy ailments and those that may require medical attention. Do not read this chapter to discover all the things that may go wrong – many things may go right. Worry is a negative emotion that achieves nothing, but to be forewarned is to be forearmed. **If you have any concerns, please discuss them directly with your medical backup team – your midwife and doctor – as they are the medical experts who are there to help you.**

To find more information about 'normal' pregnancy symptoms, and when your CO may begin to experience them, please see *Chapter 1: Raw Recruits.*

Report to the stores:

Essential equipment that you need to acquire

5

THE BRIEF

There is a huge amount of products that it is possible to buy for your BT. However, in the beginning they will actually require relatively few things. What they do need is close physical contact, food, warmth, a safe and secure environment and lots of love. You and your CO will be able to assess your BT's ongoing needs and respond accordingly. There are a set of basics that you'll need to have before you bring your BT home: beyond that, everything is a bonus. It may be prudent to wait until your CO is in her second trimester, when her pregnancy is well established, before you start to buy things.

THE OBJECTIVE

By the end of this chapter you will have an overview of all the basics that you need to buy to ensure you can meet your BT's clothing, changing, feeding, sleeping and bathing needs. There's also a list of essentials for your first aid kit, and buying tips for baby carriers, travel systems, pushchairs and car seats. That is not to say you can't buy more. If you have the funds and want to buy every gadget and gizmo available, then by all means do. But don't feel that you have to.

ADVICE FROM THE FRONT LINE

'What do you need to buy? Less than you think!'
SAM WINTERSON

'Buy everything!'
GRANT MILLS

CLOTHING

Baby troopers need to be two things: comfortable and accessible (for many nappy-changing sorties). They need stretchy, soft, warm clothes that can withstand the rigours of repeated washing. Do not underestimate the ability of your BT to generate huge amounts of washing. As a Commando Dad I am sure you already know your way around a washing machine, but if not, familiarise yourself now. Your BT will need:

- Ten babygrows and ten sleepsuits with poppers. These are practical, comfortable and easily accessible for changing nappies
- Ten sets of socks (beware, they will kick them off on a regular basis)
- Three pairs of scratch mittens to prevent your BT scratching their own face (beware, they will come off on a regular basis)
- Three cardigans or cotton jackets. Thin layers are better than very thick clothes
- Five cotton hats to keep your BT warm (a lot of heat escapes through the head). If the weather is cold, you will need a soft, warm hat for outdoor wear. Hats should be removed when your BT is indoors
- Two baby blankets, sometimes called 'receiving blankets'. These are smaller than cot blankets and are used for keeping your BT warm throughout the day

COMMANDO DAD TOP TIP

In the early days, the amount of washing a new BT generates can quickly become overwhelming. Look up launderettes in your local area so that you can fall back on them if you need to. Dropping off a bag of dirty washing and picking it up again clean, dried and folded is the nearest thing to magic I think I have ever experienced.

NAPPIES AND CHANGING KIT

- If using disposable nappies, buy the smallest bag of newborn nappies you can. You won't know if the nappies fit until your BT deploys. Even if they do, BTs grow very quickly
- If using cloth nappies, get up to speed on the different types now. Don't buy too many nappies until you know the weight of your BT
- Baby wipes or cotton wool
- Nappy rash cream
- Wipe-clean changing mat
- Nappy bags, if desired. Useful, but not essential, for 'bomb disposal'. Any small plastic bag will serve as a good alternative if you are out of nappy bags – ideally, a biodegradable one. Keep them out of reach of your BT

KITBAG

You will need a dedicated kitbag to carry around essential supplies for sorties away from base camp. It will need to contain changing and feeding kit. I advocate using a rucksack with outside pockets because they are roomy enough to fit in what you need, are comfortable to carry, easy to access and leave your arms free for your Commando Dad duties. You can use your CO's bag if you wish. For more information about kitbags and packing essential supplies, please see *Commando Dad: Basic Training*.

Here is an essential kit list for taking your newborn BT out on a sortie away from base camp:

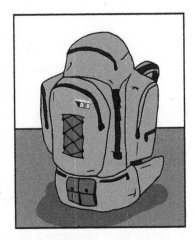

- Wipes
- Nappies
- Small pot of nappy rash cream (which also acts as a sunblock and a cream for cuts, grazes and sunburn)
- Clean dummy (if used) with cover
- Changes of clothes: at least two full sets
- Antibacterial hand gel
- Nappy bags or plastic bags
- Portable, wipe-clean changing mat (or a clean towel will suffice)
- Basic first aid kit
- Spare keys to your house/car

COMMANDO DAD TOP TIP

All contents of your basic survival kit are non-perishable. This is intentional. Clear it out often, as it will inevitably become a home for perishable items. I put the contents of my basic survival kit in a plastic bag before putting it in my rucksack. This not only protects against inclement weather and spillages, but also makes the bag easier to clear out.

FEEDING

ADVICE FROM THE FRONT LINE

'When my daughter was born, I kept a feeding record. Basically, what times the baby fed, for how long, and which breast. Early on it helped us to get used to the

routine and work out whether the baby wanted comfort, food or rest etc. Secondly, every time the nurse asked, I knew the details. That felt good.'
STUART COOPER

Breastfeeding

- A breast pump is essential if your CO plans to express breast milk. You can buy electric or manual hand pumps, depending on her preference
- Breast pads (absorbent pads that sit in the bra to absorb breastmilk that leaks)
- Nipple cream for sore, cracked nipples
- Nursing (breastfeeding) bras

Bottle feeding

- Two bottles to begin with. You will need more (eight is a good number to ensure that you always have clean bottles), but before you invest more money, you'll need to establish whether your BT will like the bottle or teat you have chosen
- Spare teats. Teats that are torn or deteriorated will need to be discarded straight away as they can harbour germs and could also make the milk flow faster than your BT is ready for
- Two bottle brushes that are only ever used for washing these bottles
- An insulated bottle carrier, if required: for times when you are out and about, without access to a cookhouse, and need to give your BT a warm bottle

Formula feeding

Correct formula for your BT's age. If you have a premature baby, they may benefit from formula milks specially designed to ensure they get the extra nutrients they need. Speak to your midwife or medical support team for advice.

Sterilisation equipment

- A saucepan (used only for this purpose) and water. You'll need to boil all parts of the bottle for ten minutes in a saucepan, but be aware that this will wear out teats quickly. You'll need to balance the costs of new nipples against the cost savings of not needing any special equipment
- An electric or microwave steam steriliser. Usually takes a few minutes and the bottles can be stored in the steriliser, keeping them sterile for hours (always check manufacturer's instructions). If you have a microwave, this is probably the most practical option
- A cold-water sterilisation solution. This allows you to soak bottles and other equipment from as little as fifteen minutes to twenty-four hours. You will need to buy sterilisation tablets or fluid regularly. Check the manufacturer's instructions to see if you'll need to rinse items before use.

SLEEPING

- A Moses basket or cot with a new, snug-fitting (i.e. a gap of no more than 2 cm) mattress. Gaps around the mattress can be dangerous. You can use a Moses basket or cot that has been used before as long as it can be thoroughly cleaned, but do not use a second-hand mattress as it may pose a health risk
- A room thermometer. The ideal temperature for your BT's room is 18°C (64°F). Set your thermostat to this temperature now so that you can get used to what this temperature actually feels like
- Baby monitors if you wish to use them
- Three cot sheets that are either fitted (with elasticated corners) or can be tucked in well
- Four thin, soft cotton blankets and two cellular blankets (i.e. blankets with holes). Layering blankets will make it easier to regulate your BT's temperature

TOP TIP

COMMANDO DAD TOP TIP

Blankets need to be in a position where your BT cannot wriggle under them or pull them over their face. Sleeping bags (once your BT is 8 lb 8 oz/3.8 kg or over) are recommended to prevent this risk.

Nursery furniture

There are many excellent bargains to be had in second-hand nursery furniture. Good places to look for second-hand furniture are classified ads in local newspapers, noticeboards in newsagents/supermarkets, eBay and Freecycle. Freecycle is an online community where unwanted belongings are given good homes (and kept out of landfill) for free. See www.freecycle.org. The National Childbirth Trust (NCT) also hold regular Nearly New Sales. Exercise normal levels of caution if buying second-hand goods.

It is also possible to rent nursery furniture. If you buy new, order for delivery at least a month before your BT is due.

- Comfortable chair (for you to sit in to feed, play with, read to, cuddle and comfort your BT)
- Soft lighting (even if it's just a small bedside lamp with a low-wattage bulb). The 'big light' used in the small hours can startle and over stimulate both of you
- Blackout blinds or thick curtains
- Changing table, if required. I preferred to use a mobile changing station, i.e. keeping all my nappy-changing kit mobile and changing my BT on an available stable and safe surface (e.g. the floor or the middle of a bed)

TOP TIP

COMMANDO DAD TOP TIP

You're going to be changing your BT a lot. Wherever you choose to do it, protect your back by making sure you don't need to lean over too much.

BATHING

- Your BTs can be washed with water alone, but if you decide to buy baby bath wash or shampoo, use it sparingly. Buy brands that will not sting if they get in the eyes
- Soft flannels and towels
- A foam or plastic bath-support that will enable you to use your bath for your BT

TOP TIP

COMMANDO DAD TOP TIP

If you choose to buy a baby bath, it will enable you to bath your BT wherever is most convenient for you. However, they are large – and will need to be stored when not in use – and will be used for a relatively short space of time. You may want to consider using a support in the bath instead.

BASIC FIRST AID KIT
Core kit

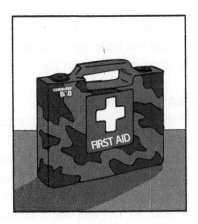

- Sachets of paediatric paracetamol and paediatric ibuprofen. If you prefer bottles, use those instead, but always keep backup sachets in your first aid kit. Check the label to ensure your trooper meets the weight and age requirements before administering. If your BT was premature, count their age from their due date
- Antiseptic cream, also suitable for stings and bites
- Antiseptic wipes
- Hypoallergenic bandages
- Hypoallergenic tape
- Hypoallergenic plasters
- Digital ear thermometer

- Baby dosing syringe (to administer the medicine)
- Tweezers
- Scissors

Useful additions (can be bought as and when needed):
- Cotton wool balls and cotton buds
- Instant cold pack, which when squeezed or shaken, the ingredients react to rapidly cool the pack. It is the equivalent of instant crushed ice
- Saline solution and eye bath
- Sachets of rehydration salts (to replace the salts and minerals lost through diarrhoea and vomiting). Only to be used on the advice of your doctor
- Calamine lotion

The following items may require you to do a bit of research beforehand to find out what works for you. It is best to do this now, as time will be in short supply when your BT deploys.

BABY CARRIER

Baby carriers are a great solution for transporting very young BTs. Baby carriers hold your BT against your body, but leave your hands free for your many other tasks. Other advantages are:

- Your BT will feel warm and secure
- The physical closeness may help you bond with each other
- When your BT is old enough to hold their head unsupported (by about six months), some models enable you to turn your BT round so they can face the world

Ease of use
- Can you fasten and unfasten the clasps easily?

Practicality
- Is it comfortable? As a general rule, the wider the straps, the better
- Is it comfortable for your BT? Your BT's head and trunk should not be unsupported in any way, but of course their arms and legs can be out of the carrier
- Are you able to easily wash it?

Value
- How often do you plan to use the carrier? Is the investment worth it?

COMMANDO DAD TOP TIP
Some areas have sling libraries where you can go along and try on a variety of baby carriers (or slings) before you decide which one to buy. Find out if there is one near you on the UK Sling Libraries Network: www.ukslinglibraries.wordpress.com.

PUSHCHAIR
A pushchair can be a big investment, but if you choose wisely it can last you until your BT is a toddler.

ADVICE FROM THE FRONT LINE
'I wish we'd been told beforehand how important the pushchair and/or pram is. We're on to our third one already and Ruby is only 5 months old! We wish we'd spent more time researching and reviewing exactly what we wanted and needed from a pushchair/pram/travel system. As first-time parents, we were slightly naive when it came to this.' PAUL HOPE

Ease of use

- Is it easy to assemble? Can you do it one-handed (you may have your BT in the other hand)?
- Is it easy to manoeuvre? Can you manoeuvre it with one hand?
- If you are tall, can you adjust the height of the handles to make the pushchair easier for you to push?

Practicality

- If it will be your primary mode of transport, does it have a basket underneath for shopping and supplies?
- Will you have to get it up and down often? How heavy is it? How bulky is it?
- Will it easily fit in your car boot or your house when it is not in use?
- Is it wider than the average shop door?

Value

Does it come with the essential 'extras' (sun visor, rain cover etc) or do you need to buy these separately?

TRAVEL SYSTEM

Travel systems are a combination of a base with wheels for the car seat and a pushchair, and usually include a carrycot (which effectively converts the pushchair into a pram).

Ease of use

- Is it easy to disassemble?
- Is it easy to manoeuvre?
- Can you adjust the height of the handles?

Practicality

- Does it meet all the criteria you would demand of each individual item?
- Does the car seat fit easily in your car?

Value

- Would you have bought all the items individually: pushchair, car seat (that may need to be replaced within a year) and carrycot?

- The pram is really only useful as a means of transport until your BT can sit up, although it may be possible to use the carrycot as a first bed for your BT
- Do all the parts come as standard or do you need to buy the car seat separately?

COMMANDO DAD TOP TIP

Pushchairs are a big investment. Consider second-hand models. Good places to look for second-hand pushchairs are classified ads in local newspapers, noticeboards in newsagents/ supermarkets, eBay and Freecycle. Exercise normal levels of caution if buying second hand. Always check the safety/roadworthiness of your purchase.

CAR SEAT

A car seat is an essential – and legal – requirement for troop transportation by car. Many hospitals will not allow you to leave with your BT if you do not have one.

Ease of use

- Can you easily get it in and out of your car? Once familiar with your child restraint, fitting should take thirty seconds. Expect it to take longer at first as you get used to how it works. Ensure you are shown how to fit the seat correctly by trained assistants when buying to make this job easier and, most importantly, safe for each journey
- Is it heavy, even without your BT in it? If it is, choose a lighter one. Your BT is only going to get heavier and this could quickly make your car seat impractical

Practicality

- Does it fit your car? Good shops will offer to fit the car seat in your car. Note how they do it. Then practise
- Does it provide your child with adequate support while giving them room to grow?

- Is it safe? Does it conform to British Standards and carry the BSI 'Kitemark' or the European 'CE' mark?
- Can you remove the covers and wash them?

Value

- How long will your trooper be able to use the model you are considering?
- Hand-me-down car seats from friends and relatives are fine provided they have never been damaged (or been involved in a car accident). Also, check that they conform to the standards as mentioned above and no parts are missing. If the instructions have been lost, request replacements from the manufacturer to ensure you are familiar with how it works. If in doubt, seek professional advice

RECAP AND REFRESH

Chapter 5: Report to the stores has provided information on:

- The essentials that you need to buy for your BT. Do not feel you are limited to buying only these items, but be aware that if you buy more than you need, your base camp may end up full of kit that is surplus to requirements. Not a smart Commando Dad move
- The basics for a first aid kit
- Tips on how to buy essential equipment

Deployment day

THE BRIEF

Deployment day has arrived. Today you will need to master the art of being very, very productive while remaining very, very calm. You need to be guided by your CO as what she needs from you may change from minute to minute. You are her emotional backup support and as important to her as the medical team. She needs to stay 100% focussed on delivering your BT, a huge emotional and physical task. You need to be calm, reassuring and encouraging in everything you do, and make her as comfortable – and comforted – as you possibly can.

Gentlemen, if there's one bit of advice I can offer you today it is this: expect the unexpected.

THE OBJECTIVE

By the end of this chapter you will know how you can tell when your CO is in labour and what to do about it, from timing contractions to decamping to the hospital; the stages of labour and the telltale physical signs; and what you can expect in the delivery ward. The next chapter covers what happens after the deployment, or birth.

Remember that even if you prepared a birth plan, it may need to change to keep pace with fast-moving events. Certain facilities may not be available, or there may be complications, or your CO may simply change her mind. If the latter is the case, ensure that your CO does not waste any energy on disappointment or worse, guilt. The best possible outcome in labour is a healthy CO and BT and whichever way you get there is the right way.

TOP TIP

COMMANDO DAD TOP TIP

Be aware that, as first-time parents, you and your CO are going to meet people who want to share their nightmare scenarios of labour – in detail. Where possible, try to focus on your own journey rather than reflecting on theirs. The fact is every birth is different. As a dad to three troopers I can testify that no two births are the same. You need to be realistic about labour and childbirth: it's not going to be all good and it's not going to be all bad, but it's almost certainly going to get ugly. But you will have a medical support team on hand to give your CO all the help she needs.

ADVICE FROM THE FRONT LINE

'There is something about telling other people that you (as a couple) are expecting that seems to compel them to tell you some terrible horror story about their experience of birth/hospitals/labour. You need to try to ignore these people – they mean well, but they're actually causing worry.'

NICK BURBIDGE

PREPARATION AND PLANNING
Blood, sweat and tears

Before you get to the delivery room, you need to prepare yourself for labour, both physically and mentally. To do this, you need to be aware of the following things:

- Labour is an intense emotional and physical experience for your CO. It is inevitable that you are going to see her in pain and at times you may feel helpless. Be reassured that she is in safe hands. If you do have questions or concerns about how the labour is going, speak to one of the medical team immediately. You are your CO's mouthpiece – make sure you've discussed the 'what ifs' beforehand

- Labour can take a long time and it is easy to lose track of time. Make sure you grab opportunities you can to eat, drink and nap. You need to take care of your personal admin so that you can take care of your CO and bring her whatever she needs
- There is going to be a lot more blood – and other bodily fluids – than you might imagine
- The most effective way to push a baby out is 'bearing down' – the same downward pushing that we use on the loo. Your BT may not be the first thing to deploy.
- Your BT is going to be born with a blue tinge and will be sticky and wet with amniotic fluid, blood and vernix caseosa, a white, waxy substance that protected their skin during pregnancy
- The umbilical cord, that attached your BT to your CO, is a thick, blue-greyish, twisted cord with the consistency of gristle
- The placenta, or afterbirth, needs to be delivered after your BT. It will be bloody and purple-grey, with the consistency of raw meat or liver
- Nothing can prepare you for the range of emotions you will feel when your BT deploys – it is indescribable

ADVICE FROM THE FRONT LINE

'If labour is a long affair, prepare to feel more useless than you've ever felt before.'
JOHN ALLEN

'The medical team was excellent ... they do everything they can to help. My biggest tip would be never to be afraid to ask them for help or advice.'
PAUL DRAKE

COMMANDO DAD TOP TIP

What happens in the delivery room, stays in the delivery room. I was a commando, but was never exposed to half of the words my CO threw at me during labour. But I didn't take it personally – and neither should you.

LABOUR

Signs that labour may be on its way

- As your CO's body prepares for labour, she may notice the following, or she may not. There is no one single set of signs to look out for:
- Nesting instinct: a desire to clean, tidy and even move furniture or decorate your base camp
- A sudden rush of energy
- Increased irritability or mood swings
- 'Lightening', when your BT drops down into her pelvis ready for birth. She may experience this as being able to breathe more easily

CALL THE MEDIC

If your CO shows the signs of labour below prior to 37 weeks, get her emergency medical assistance. She may be in premature labour.

How to recognise labour

You and your CO may not immediately recognise that labour has started. Look out for the following:

- Your CO passes a mucus plug, a brown or pink tinged, jelly-like substance that has plugged the cervix shut and kept bacteria and infection out of the uterus while your BT has been developing. This does not necessarily signal the immediate onset of labour, just that the cervix has started to make changes. For some COs, labour could still be hours, days or even two weeks away
- Contractions. Late in pregnancy, your CO may have experienced

practise contractions, called Braxton Hicks. 'Real' contractions differ from these in the following ways:

- They don't go away. Early contractions may feel like persistent back pain and a crampy period pain
- Your CO may be able to feel contractions all over, not just at the front
- Although they may be irregular to start with, they will get stronger, occur at increasingly shorter intervals, last longer and become more painful
- The pain will come in a wave, reaching a peak, and then tailing off
- Your CO's waters may break. The sac of amniotic fluid your BT's been protected and nourished by breaks and the fluid drains out. This is more likely to be a trickle (as your BT's head is now resting in the pelvis and preventing much fluid escaping, almost like a plug) but it can be a gush. There is no rule about when waters break – it may occur much later in labour and sometimes they are broken in hospital by the midwife or doctor. You will need to let your midwife know if your CO's waters have broken though as without the amniotic fluid, your BT is less protected against infection
- Upset stomach/diarrhoea. Your CO's body will release prostaglandins in early labour to help contractions and to soften and dilate the cervix. In some instances, these can stimulate her bowels

How to time the contractions

You will need a way to accurately time seconds: get a watch with a second hand or use the stopwatch on your phone.

- Time the frequency of contractions from the *beginning* of one to the *beginning* of the next. This will include the actual contraction and the rest time in between
- Your midwife will need to know the frequency of contractions to determine whether you need to take your CO to the hospital
- If contractions are painful and last thirty seconds or more, your CO is likely to be in labour

If you have any doubts about whether your CO's labour is starting, call your midwife for guidance. Ideally, your CO will need to speak to the midwife, not only because she can answer the questions about how she is feeling directly, but also the midwife will be able to discern a lot from the tone of her voice and how she is coping with contractions.

The general rule is:

- If the contractions are five minutes apart, it's time to get your CO to hospital
- If contractions are two minutes or less apart, call for medical backup and prepare yourself: you may need to deliver your BT. See 'Emergency deployment' in *Chapter 8: When things* don't *go to plan.*

ADVICE FROM THE FRONT LINE

'During labour it is important to admin yourself – take on food and water even if you don't feel like it and take any opportunities to sleep. You are no use to your CO if you keel over from dehydration or lack of food. The hospital staff will look after your CO's admin, you are responsible for your own.'

NEIL WHITE

Decamping to the hospital

Unless either of you are concerned, or your CO feels she cannot cope at home for much longer, staying at home is the best option in the early stages of labour. This is not only because you are likely to be sent home from the hospital (as the early stage of labour can be a long, gradual process), which will be frustrating for both of you, but also because it is easier for your CO to be comfortable at home.

In early labour, where possible, help your CO to:

- Rest, especially if her labour starts during the night. Challenging when the most momentous event to ever happen in your lives is imminent, but energy saved now will help later
- Focus on something else. Again, challenging. But it may help the time pass a little faster
- Take gentle exercise. A gentle walk and stretching – nothing too strenuous – may help the labour progress
- Relieve discomfort: your CO may want to move her body instinctively in time with her contractions, or do some of her pregnancy exercises. A warm bath or shower may also help
- Drink. Your CO's body is working very hard and needs to be kept hydrated for the job ahead. Frequent urination will also help as an empty bladder leaves more room for your BT to descend
- Eat. If your CO can face food (she may feel sick or have an upset stomach) it will help keep her energy levels up. Light, easily digested food is the best option
- Relax. Do anything you can to reduce any stress and anxiety your CO may be experiencing. Be guided by her

 ADVICE FROM THE FRONT LINE

'Be supportive and don't panic. Let the midwives do their job. They are very good at it. Whatever your CO asks of you at the time, do it to the best of your ability. Whilst I was coming out with all the encouragements I could, my wife said I wasn't helping. So I asked, "What would you like me to do?" She said hold her hand and smile like everything was going to be OK. And that's what I did. She felt better about that and so did I. You are not the best judge when it comes to labour – your CO is – so let them dictate the event.' JAMES FENWICK

Speak to your midwife beforehand about when your CO will need to head into hospital. This will depend on a number of factors including how regular and long her contractions are, and how long it is going to take you to get there. As a rule of thumb, if your CO's contractions have been regular for an hour, are about five minutes apart and lasting between 45–60 seconds, it's time to call the midwife or hospital. She may be in the active phase of the first stage of labour. See 'The stages of labour' below for more details.

 ADVICE FROM THE FRONT LINE

'Just before our first BT was due, the weather was turning – it started to snow – but we did not anticipate how much! My partner went into labour and we could not get the car out of the snow and onto the road. Even the ambulance took over 45 minutes to arrive due to snow! So my tip would be to prepare for such weather events before labour. Make sure you call the midwife in time – don't leave it so late that help can't get to you on time.'

JACK CARTER

THE STAGES OF LABOUR

There are three stages of labour:

Stage 1: Contractions begin and your CO's cervix dilates to 10 cm. Split into three phases:

- Early (or 'latent')
- Active
- Transitional

Stage 2: The pushing stage and birth

Stage 3: Your CO delivers the afterbirth

STAGE 1: Your CO's body prepares for your BT's birth

How long will it last? This is typically the longest stage of labour, and lasts from 6–12 hours on average.

What happens? Your CO's contractions open up her cervix, ready for your BT to be born. It is divided into three phases:

Early labour

Dilation: 0–4 cm

Contractions: Gradually become regular: 40–60 seconds long and 3–5 minutes apart

What happens: Your CO's cervix gradually thins out (effaces) and opens (dilates)

This is also known as the latent phase and can sometimes go on for hours and hours, and perhaps even days.

Active labour

Dilation: 4–8cm

Contractions: From 40–60 seconds long, up to 5 minutes apart, to 60 + seconds long, 2–3 minutes apart

What happens:

- Your CO's cervix begins to dilate more rapidly, and contractions are longer, stronger and closer together
- You will need to head to the hospital if you haven't already
- Once at the hospital, help your CO practise her breathing and relaxation techniques to combat her growing discomfort
- Depending on how your CO is coping with contractions, you may need to be her advocate and communicate her birth plan and pain relief wishes at the hospital, bearing in mind that you both need to go into labour with an open mind and be flexible enough to adapt if the situation requires it

Transitional labour

Dilation: 8–10 cm (fully dilated)

Contractions: 60–90 seconds long and 2–3 minutes apart

What happens:

- Your CO may feel shaky and sick as there is a final surge in hormones and adrenalin to give her the energy to push. There's a lot of discharge at this stage – bloody and other fluids – and she may vomit
- As your CO's cervix fully dilates, your BT's head will probably have descended into her pelvis, giving her a feeling of pressure in her rectum
- Your CO may have an overwhelming urge to push. You must help your CO understand and follow the midwife's instructions, as her cervix may not be fully dilated and so she should not push. If she does, she may tire herself with unproductive pushing. She needs to save energy where she can

If your CO has had an epidural, she may experience this phase differently. If she wants to actively take part in the next stage, she can ask to have her epidural dose lowered at the end of transition. She should speak to her midwife or doctor beforehand about the pros and cons of this approach.

 ADVICE FROM THE FRONT LINE

'I never knew my wife had such a strong grip until her contractions started. Put it this way, I'll never play the piano again! The worst thing was seeing my wife in pain and distress – not something we want to see happen to our CO, but remember she is in safe and professional hands in the hospital environment and you have to put your faith and trust in them and let them do their job.' CALUM BEATT

STAGE 2: Your CO gives birth

How long will it last? Anything from a few minutes to a few hours.

What happens? This is the pushing stage, when your CO delivers your BT.

- Your midwife will confirm that the cervix is fully open and your CO can push. She may have to guide your CO when to push – and when to stop

- Your CO may want to use the breathing techniques she has learned in antenatal classes between pushes – help her to remember them

- As your BT's head emerges or 'crowns', your CO may experience an intense stinging or burning sensation; reassure her she is nearly there. It is critical that you help your CO follow the midwife's instructions now, as she may need to stop pushing to avoid a tear in her perineum and help the midwife ease the baby's head out gently, but she may still be experiencing an overwhelming urge to push

- Your midwife may need to perform an episiotomy (i.e. cut your CO's perineum) to help your BT be delivered

- Once your BT's head is delivered, your midwife will ensure the umbilical cord is free

- Once your BT's head is delivered, it will rotate to the side as their shoulders get in position for delivery

- Your midwife will guide out the shoulders (the widest part of your BT) one at a time and the rest of your BT will be born shortly afterwards

- After a quick visual check (Apgar test) and a brisk wipe down, your CO will be able to hold your new BT in her arms or on her abdomen, depending on the length of the umbilical cord

- The umbilical cord can be clamped and cut now or, if you and your CO prefer, after the cord has stopped pulsating. This is known as a physiological third stage. The cord can be cut by you or the midwife depending on your preference. You may need to remind the midwife if you want to cut the cord

- Following a brief examination by your midwife or doctor, your BT will be weighed, measured and given two ID wristbands with your CO's name on

TOP TIP

COMMANDO DAD TOP TIP

Cutting the cord: The umbilical cord is a thick, twisted cord with the consistency of gristle. If you intend to cut it, be aware that it won't be a matter of a quick snip. Be reassured that neither your CO nor your BT will feel a thing, no matter how long it takes.

STAGE 3: Your CO delivers the afterbirth

How long will it last? Typically, between five and thirty minutes.

What happens? Your CO gives birth to the placenta, your BT's life support system for the past nine months. It is now referred to as the afterbirth.

- Your CO will have contractions, although much milder
- Your midwife may massage her abdomen to help encourage the body to deliver the afterbirth, and your CO may need to push. To further help the delivery, your midwife may offer your CO an injection of a synthetic form of oxytocin – the hormone that naturally makes the uterus contract – known as Syntocin. There will be more blood as the afterbirth is delivered
- Your midwife will examine the afterbirth to ensure it's intact. Any fragments that are left inside the uterus will need to be removed to prevent bleeding or infection
- If your CO did tear, or had an episiotomy, your midwife will give her stitches
- Your midwife may rub your CO's abdomen, directly beneath her belly button, to help her uterus contract and keep any bleeding in check. If your CO can breastfeed this will also help her uterus contract

ADVICE FROM THE FRONT LINE

'I was not prepared for the mess in the labour room. My wife only lost about 500 ml blood but the place looked like a scene from CSI by the time we were finished. It was a surreal experience having to wipe her blood from my shoes at the end of the evening.'
NEIL WHITE

PAIN RELIEF

People have all sorts of ideas and opinions about pain relief during labour and delivery, but there is only one person in the world who can ultimately make the decision: your CO. She needs to discuss pain relief options with her midwife (with your support) in order to gather the information she needs to make a judgement. She needs to explore what's available beforehand. Remember: it is your CO's choice to discuss options for pain relief at all stages of her labour, but it may reduce her stress levels if she is fully informed of her options beforehand.

ADVICE FROM THE FRONT LINE

'My wife went into the hospital wanting just gas and air, but that quickly changed. Knowing about the different pain relief options helped as I had to help her make the decisions, particularly when things were moving quickly. I had to tell the midwife that she would take morphine as she couldn't actually speak at that point.'
NEIL WHITE

Here you will find a brief overview of the pain relief available, and the pros and cons to consider. You and your CO will need to speak to your midwife for more information and to discuss your specific circumstances in order to make an informed decision.

Type		Method
Natural pain relief can help relax your CO, help to ease her pain and make contractions more bearable	Heat	A hot-water bottle filled with hot (but not boiling) water on the lower back
	Water	A hot (not too hot): • shower, with the shower head trained on your CO's lower back • bath
	Breathing	• Your CO can learn some rhythmic breathing techniques for labour, which won't remove the pain, but will make it more manageable
	Massage	• A massage can help your CO's body release endorphins – a natural 'feel good' hormone. But be guided by your CO – she may not want to be touched at all, or only touched gently.
	Position	• If your CO lies on her back it can make her contractions slower and more painful – try to encourage and support her to walk around and use upright positions. She may also find squatting, being on all fours, kneeling on a chair or using a birthing ball can help • She may find lying on her side can help her rest and will not compress any major veins in her body • Her midwife will give advice on the best positions for birth
	TENS machine	• A TENS (transcutaneous electrical nerve stimulation) machine sends off small electrical impulses that encourage your CO's body to produce endorphins, a natural painkiller. It will be attached to your CO via sticky pads on her back

	Pros	Cons
Gas and air A mixture of oxygen and nitrous oxide gas, self-administered by your CO via a mask or mouthpiece	Reduces pain and makes it more bearable	Won't remove all the pain
	Your CO can control it herself	It may make your CO feel light-headed and nauseous
	Provides instant relief	
	It is possible to ask for a painkilling injection if you need more pain relief	
Pethidine – or other opiate – injection Administered by an injection in the muscles of your CO's buttocks or thigh	Reduces pain and may help your CO relax, and therefore rest	Won't remove all the pain
		It may make your CO feel light-headed or dizzy and nauseous
	It shouldn't slow your CO's labour down if she is already in active labour	It may make it difficult for your CO to push
		There's a timing issue. If given too soon before the birth it may affect your BT's breathing and make them drowsy for up to a few days and/or effect your BT's sucking and rooting reflexes, making it more difficult to breastfeed
Epidural Painkilling drugs are passed into the small of your CO's back via a fine tube that is inserted using a long, hollow needle	The most effective form of pain relief, working for the majority of women	There's a timing issue: • Too soon and it may slow down labour • Too late and it will not have time to take affect before your BT is deployed
	Serious side effects are rare	Side effects that your CO may experience include a severe headache, numbness, itching, fever, shivering or a sudden drop in blood pressure (in which case your CO may need a drip)
	Your CO will be monitored closely if she has an epidural so if she does need help, she will get it quickly	Your CO is more likely to need help speeding labour up using drugs, as an epidural can slow labour
		The second stage of labour – pushing – may take longer and your CO may not feel the urge to push. This may mean that your CO needs an assisted birth – e.g. forceps or a ventouse
		After delivery, your CO will need to rest until the effects of the anaesthetic have passed. She may not be able to feel or move her legs properly for several hours. She may also need a catheter (a tube into her bladder that will drain away her pee) as she may not realise when her bladder is full

INDUCTION

Your CO may be offered an induction, where labour is started artificially. This may be because she is past 42 weeks pregnant or the medical team feel there may be a risk to your CO or BT's health. You can discuss this directly with the doctor or midwife when it is suggested. It is up to your CO whether she has her labour induced or not. If your CO is induced, she is statistically more likely to need an epidural or other pain relief as induced labour is generally more painful than labour that starts on its own.

ADVICE FROM THE FRONT LINE

'One thing that no one explained to me was what an induction was. My wife was induced and until that point, I thought an induction was a chance for us to go to the ward, meet the nurses and get comfortable with the surroundings. I got a big shock when I realised that this was not the case.'

NEIL WHITE

Membrane sweep

If you do decide to have labour induced, your CO should first be offered a 'membrane sweep' or 'cervical sweep' to bring on labour.

Your CO's midwife or doctor will sweep their finger around your CO's cervix to loosen it from the amniotic sac. The separation releases prostaglandins that may kick-start your CO's labour. It shouldn't hurt your CO, but it will be uncomfortable. There may be some bleeding afterwards.

If the membrane sweep doesn't work, your CO will be offered an induction using a synthetic form of prostaglandins. She will need to have a tablet, gel or pessary inserted directly into her vagina. Although she needs to go to the hospital maternity unit for this, depending on the policy of your hospital, you may be allowed to go home and wait for labour to begin. Ask your midwife how long the induction will take to work. Some pessaries are controlled release and may take up to twenty-four hours to take effect. Others are expected to work within hours, and if they haven't, your midwife or doctor will need to perform an examination to see if your CO requires further prostaglandins.

 ADVICE FROM THE FRONT LINE

'My wife had the dream pregnancy, but had to be induced in the end. That's when it went a bit wrong and all our preparations went flying out the window. As a result, our first month was very rocky. Thankfully our son is 6 months now and is fighting fit. We are loving every minute of parenthood, but there can be a dark side that we all need to acknowledge so things are made easier.'
JAMES WICKHAM

PLANNING AND PREPARATION PREVENT POOR PARENTAL PERFORMANCE

Prior to deployment day, you need to know:
- Your route to hospital, at different times of the day, and alternatives
- If you don't drive, the number of a very reliable taxi company or a friend or relative who will be on standby
- How to accurately time contractions
- The route to and the layout of your local hospital. Where the maternity ward is, and A&E, in relation to the car park
- The best parking spaces and how you are going to pay for parking (see below)
- Important contact numbers (put them in your phone)

- If you have pets, someone to look after them. You'll need to have someone on standby to feed and take care of them when you leave for the hospital and in those first few disjointed days

You need to ensure:
- Your car always has at least enough petrol to get to and from the hospital
- You have an 'Emergency deployment' kit in the car, in case you don't make it to the hospital in time. Read 'Emergency deployment' in *Chapter 8: When things don't go to plan* for more information about how to cope in this situation. Your kit will need to include:
  - Blankets and towels, clean and sealed in a large plastic bag (to prevent them getting dirty in your car). You can use the empty plastic bag to store the placenta in until your emergency backup team can get to you
  - Head torch ideally, or normal torch, with batteries
  - Hand sanitiser and/or sterile gloves
  - Bottles of water, sports drinks and high-energy snacks for your CO

You need to take:
- Change for hospital parking and vending machines
- Camera (but be sure to ask if and when you are allowed to take pictures. Some hospitals don't allow pictures in the delivery room, for example)
- Phone and charger – make sure you have pre-programmed the numbers of all the people you need to inform about the BT's arrival. If you've got a lot of people to tell, you might also want to consider finding a friend or family member who you can call with the good news, and let them cascade it far and wide. However, you must tell the new grandparents yourself. This is a life-changing moment for them, too
- Your CO's hospital bag
- Water and high-energy snacks

FOOTNOTE

Congratulations – your BT is here. Your CO did it – she is amazing. You need to make sure she knows it. Hopefully your planning and preparation paid off and the delivery went as well as it could. If it didn't, hopefully you were prepared enough to roll with the punches because you were armed with the knowledge that there is no such thing as a textbook delivery. It's worth saying again: the best outcome for deployment day is a healthy CO and BT and whichever way you get there is the right way.

EMOTION ALERT

Incoming! Gentlemen, expect waves of huge emotions.

RECAP AND REFRESH

Chapter 6: Deployment day has provided the following information:
- Signs that labour may be on its way
- How to recognise labour
- How to time contractions
- When to leave for the hospital
- The stages of labour
- Pain relief options
- Induction

- If you want more information about what happens to your CO and BT after the birth, please see *Chapter 7: What happens next*
- For information about emergency deployment (if you need to deliver your BT without professional assistance), Caesarean section, assisted delivery or if your BT needs special care, please see *Chapter 8: When things don't go to plan*
- If your CO is expecting twins or multiples, please see the 'Multiple

deployments' section in *Chapter 9: Special ops*

- If your CO wants to give birth at home or at a midwife-led unit, please see the relevant sections in *Chapter 9: Special ops*
- If your CO wants a natural (i.e. medication-free) birth, please see the 'Natural childbirth' section in *Chapter 9: Special ops*
- If you are a young dad (16–24), please see the 'Young Commando Dads' section in *Chapter 9: Special ops*

7

What
happens next

THE BRIEF

The moment that you and your CO have been preparing for – labour and childbirth – is now complete. You both have a new little life to take care of and it's now time for the next phase of your fatherhood adventure to begin.

THE OBJECTIVE

By the end of this chapter, you will understand what happens from the moment you and your CO are handed your BT to the moment you are able to take them back to base camp.

You can get more information about the subjects covered in this chapter – picking up and holding your BT; changing both disposable and non-disposable nappies; cleaning; feeding and all the associated administration; and burping your BT – in the videos on the 'Surviving the first 24 hours' section under *Resources* on the Commando Dad website: www.commandodad.com. You can also find more information on these skills and guidance on baby-proofing your base camp and cleaning your BT's stump – what's left of the umbilical cord – in *Commando Dad: Basic Training*, a book designed to provide you with all the skills you need to be an effective hands-on dad.

HOLDING YOUR BT

Your BT does not have the strength to support their own head and so you must take great care to support it for them.

- To pick up your BT, you will need to slide your hands under their head and bottom and lift their whole body
- If your BT is handed to you, put one hand under their head and another under their body. If the first time you hold your BT is after the birth, be aware that they will be very slippery
- To sit with your BT, rest their head in the crook of your arm or hold them against your shoulder, with one hand supporting their head and neck and the other supporting their bottom

TOP TIP

COMMANDO DAD TOP TIP

Make sure there is nothing in the vicinity that you can trip on. Sounds obvious, but holding your newborn BT can have an almost hypnotic effect upon you, making you oblivious to what's around you.

FEEDING

Health experts agree that breast milk is best for your BT and you and your CO will both know the benefits of breastfeeding from your antenatal classes. However, just because it is natural, doesn't necessarily mean that it comes naturally. It is a skill that often needs to be learned. And remember that your BT is learning it too.

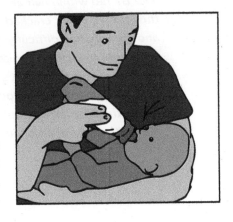

If your CO does intend to breastfeed, ideally the best time to start is just after birth. Your BT is likely to be alert and their feeding reflexes – rooting and sucking – are strong. Breastfeeding at this point (even if she doesn't intend to breastfeed moving forward) will also help your CO produce the hormone that will help her deliver the placenta and contract her uterus (which may help with blood loss). If your CO had pethidine or another opiate painkiller, your BT may be drowsy, affecting their sucking and rooting reflexes.

Some COs find breastfeeding comes easily. However, if your CO does experience difficulties, she should never, ever feel that she is a failure. It is a basic human instinct to provide food for our young and it can be frustrating and upsetting if she feels that she is unable to. There are people on hand who can offer help and advice: midwives, health visitors and local support groups. The fact that there are so many people on hand to help shows that lots of women benefit from help and support with breastfeeding. Whatever works for you and your family is the right thing to do.

ADVICE FROM THE FRONT LINE

'Our BT fed within half an hour of being born and we thought we had it cracked. She then changed her mind and my wife had difficulty getting her latched on. We were able to stay in hospital until my wife felt as though she had mastered it. That's a good point to consider and isn't often mentioned – you don't always have to rush out of the hospital and get stressed at home, you can stay with the professionals until you are ready to leave.'
STEVE COOPER

TOP TIP

COMMANDO DAD TOP TIP

Take the opportunity to attend a breastfeeding class before your BT is born. Do not leave it until the first feed to find out what needs to be done because at that point, everyone involved is likely to be tired and emotional.

ADVICE FROM THE FRONT LINE

'If your baby is struggling to latch on, or appears to eat very little and often, ask the health visitor to check for a tongue-tie that may have been missed. '

JOHN ALLEN

Whether or not to breastfeed is a hugely emotive subject and your CO needs to make the ultimate decision. If she does decide to breastfeed, you will need to offer the following practical support:

- Make sure she has the equipment she needs: breast pads, nipple cream, clean nursing bras, burp cloths (also known as muslins) and a breast pump and bottles if she plans to express
- If she plans to express, learn how to clean, sterilise and make up a bottle of breast milk. Then take the opportunity to feed your BT. If possible, take the night feeds, enabling your CO to get as much unbroken sleep as possible. She needs to recover from the birth
- Learn how to store expressed breast milk for later use
- Back at base camp, make sure she has a comfortable place to breastfeed
- Make sure she eats wholesome food and drinks enough. Breast-feeding can burn an extra 500 calories a day. See *Chapter 3: Fit for fatherhood* for nutrition tips. You need to look after your CO, so that she can nourish your BT

- After your CO has fed your BT, you can burp or 'wind' them. Burping needs to come after every feed and is important as it prevents painful trapped wind.
- Take the initiative on household chores, which will now also include a lot of washing. This will allow your CO to focus on breastfeeding without having to worry that she needs to be doing something else

ADVICE FROM THE FRONT LINE

'Do not underestimate the role of millions of years of evolution and ignore your instinct. We found that my wife's gut feeling about how the baby wanted to breastfeed was exactly the right thing to do.'
STEVE COOPER

If she does decides to bottle feed, you will need to offer the following practical support:

- Make sure she has the equipment she needs: bottles, age-appropriate formula, burp cloths, equipment to effectively clean and sterilise bottles, a ready supply of clean and sterilised bottles
- Learn bottle administration – how to clean, sterilise and make up a bottle of formula
- Take the opportunity to feed, and burp, your BT. If possible, take the night feeds, enabling your CO to get as much unbroken sleep as possible

ADVICE FROM THE FRONT LINE

'We found the whole breastfeeding thing difficult to cope with. My partner wasn't producing enough milk, but the hospital experience is so single-mindedly focussed on breastfeeding that it was difficult to get someone to really listen to us. Your partner will really know what is and isn't working and don't be afraid to challenge the dogmatic approach to breastfeeding. She'll also need lots of support because this status quo can result in women feeling like they have somehow failed – which, of course, they haven't!'

NICK BURBRIDGE

'The first few months of feeding was like hell for us. The best advice we got and would give to any new parents is "do what feels right for you" whether it's breast or bottle. When you do that, everything falls into place for a much happier unit.'

DANIEL SAXTON

WHEN YOU ARE ASKED TO LEAVE THE HOSPITAL

Be aware that, following birth, your CO and new BT will be transferred onto the maternity ward and you will need to leave the hospital. This may be sooner than any of you are ready for. The best thing you can do is go back to base camp, get some sleep if possible and ensure that the next day you're waiting outside your CO's ward when visiting hours commence.

ADVICE FROM THE FRONT LINE

'My wife and newborn BT were taken away from me and I was told to go home. Wow. I did not expect or even know this would happen. I was gutted. However, they were well looked after. My CO and BT needed their rest, and so did I.'

JAMES FENWICK

When it is time for you to leave, you will very probably be sleep deprived and almost certainly buzzing with adrenaline. You may not be operating at your normal mental capacity. Be careful.

ADVICE FROM THE FRONT LINE

'I got totally lost on my drive home, even though I should have known the way. I was totally exhausted and mentally drained. In effect, we went without sleep for 2 days (labour started one night and our BT was born the following day).'

SAM WINTERSON

TOP TIP

COMMANDO DAD TOP TIP

Find out beforehand your hospital's policies and procedures for allowing new dads to stay after the birth of their BTs, and also visiting times, number of people allowed etc. Make sure you have the number for the maternity ward in case you need or want to get in touch.

CHANGING NAPPIES

You may be there for your BT's first dirty nappy, which will appear within the first twenty-four hours after birth, or you may not. Luckily, there will be plenty of opportunity for you to get hands-on experience in the months and years to come.

ADVICE FROM THE FRONT LINE

'If, like me, you struggle with the first nappy, don't worry. Within weeks you will be nappy-changing like a pro.'
DAN SAXTON

There are three stages to your BT's poos, or stools:

- **Meconium stools:** Meconium forms from materials ingested in the uterus. It will appear in your BT's nappy within the first twenty-four hours and for the first two–three days. It is very sticky and dark green. The best way to describe it is as a tar-like glue
- **Transition stools:** this is the stage between meconium and 'normal' stools. They are looser and lighter in colour
- **Milk stools:** start to appear about day six
  - Breastfed BTs: Light mustard colour, they may have a slightly sweet smell. They can still be loose in texture
  - Bottle-fed (formula) BTs: Pale yellow or brown, they will have a strong smell and have a thicker texture

Bowel habits in newborns can be slightly irregular, but as long as their stools are soft and pass easily there shouldn't be a problem. Be aware that bottle-fed babies are more prone to constipation as formula is not as easily digested as breast milk. If you have any questions or concerns, speak to your midwife or health visitor.

For a video showing how to change a disposable and a non-disposable nappy, go to the 'Surviving the first 24 hours' section under *Resources* on the Commando Dad website: www.commandodad.com.

COMMANDO DAD TOP TIP

What's left of the umbilical cord – henceforth referred to as the stump – will remain attached to your BT for a week or two, before it drops off naturally to reveal their bellybutton. In the meantime, you will need to keep the stump dry and clean, to prevent infection. You will need to clean the stump every time you change a nappy. Speak to your midwife or health visitor for more advice, or see *Commando Dad: Basic Training*.

BRINGING YOUR CO AND BT BACK TO BASE CAMP

Before you bring your BT back to base camp, you will need to have done the following:

- Ensured base camp is safe and baby-proofed. You won't need baby gates straight away – actually, they can become an unnecessary hindrance to nocturnal missions in the early days – unless you have a pet, in which case you will need to keep them apart from your BT from day one. However, it is prudent to do the rest of your baby-proofing before you bring your BT home, while you have time to do it. This will include getting covers for unused plug sockets, catches for low cupboards and protective edges for any sharp corners on furniture (you might also want to consider removing furniture with really sharp edges) and fixtures and fittings. If you have a working fireplace, you'll need a fireguard – this is a legal requirement. It will be one less thing to worry about and also give you time to get used to the changes yourself. The catches on the cupboards in particular take some getting used to, so from now on, keep the things you use less often in your low cupboards
- Assigned specific areas for necessary equipment, from nappies to pushchairs. With sleep in short supply over the next few weeks and months, you're going to want to ensure that your base camp is well

ordered, with essentials easy to find but packed neatly away
- Ensure you have stocked up on nappies, taking care not to buy too many until you know your BT's size
- Ensure you have cotton wool or wipes to clean your BT when changing

You will need to have the following:
- A car seat that conforms to safety standards if you intend to drive
- A baby carrier if you intend to walk from the hospital
- A suitable set of clothes to dress your BT in

Clothes for bringing your BT home from hospital

Your BT will need soft, breathable and accessible clothes. Cotton is best. Hands, feet and head will need to be kept covered as BTs' extremities easily get cold (and a huge amount of body heat can escape through their head). As a general rule, your BT will require one more layer of clothes than you do, unless the weather is very hot.

An ideal suit for bringing a BT back from the hospital would be:
- A babygrow, a sleepsuit, a hat, socks and scratch mittens – all in cotton
- If cold, you may need a baby blanket or two
- If very cold, you may require a snowsuit, but you will need to ensure that if you are using a car seat, your BT can be strapped in securely without causing discomfort

YOUR CO AFTER BIRTH

Your CO's physical and emotional journey of pregnancy does not end with the birth of your BT. As you will see from the list below, she will now have to go through the process of healing. Depending on whether she needed medical or surgical intervention during labour, be aware that full recovery may take weeks. Even with no intervention, she will be very sore and tender.

Your midwife or doctor can provide you with advice about painkillers your CO can take, based on your personal circumstances, and taking all of the normal precautions. In addition to pain medication, there are practical actions that you can take to help her:

- **Tenderness in the perineum:** this whole area stretched to allow your BT to be delivered and there may be a great deal of discomfort as the tissues in this area heal and slowly return to shape. This may be particularly painful if your CO's tissues sustained damage and needed stitches, either through a tear, an episiotomy or an assisted birth. Your CO may have been given ice packs at the hospital to reduce swelling and you can use them at home too, although if your CO has stitches they should ideally not be used for longer than five minutes at a time as they will start to reduce blood flow to the area and possibly hamper the recovery. To make sitting down more comfortable for your CO, get her a V-shaped cushion. These are sometimes called back support or orthopaedic cushions and are widely available. Do not use a rubber ring as this will actually increase the pressure – and therefore the discomfort – on the very area that you're attempting to relieve. Encourage your CO to avoid standing for too long as again, this will increase the pressure in the perineal area

MEDIC: STAND BY

Call your medical support team if the pain in your CO's stitches doesn't ease. It may be that the stitches are too tight or she has an infection.

- **Haemorrhoids (piles):** your CO may have developed haemorrhoids during pregnancy or while she was pushing during labour. The treatment of them is very similar to that for the perineum (see above). In addition, your CO should avoid dry toilet paper and instead use moistened wipes, specifically designed to soothe haemorrhoids. She will need to check with her midwife about using haemorrhoid suppositories. This may not be possible if she has been given stitches during labour

- **Constipation:** your CO may be constipated for a few days after giving birth. This may be because of her nervousness about going for a poo with haemorrhoids, bruising and stitches to contend with. It may also be a result of hormonal changes, her digestive system slowing down during labour and/or pain relief that she may have had during delivery. Try to make sure you provide her with plenty of fluids and high-fibre, wholegrain foods to eat

- **Afterpains:** contractions that your CO will feel as her uterus begins to shrink down to its original size. To put this into perspective, the uterus stretched over nine months, but your CO's body will return it back to shape over as little as six weeks. Breastfeeding may also exacerbate this problem, as it encourages her uterus to contract. Typically, the worst of the pain should fade after a few days. In the meantime, a warm hot water bottle can help, or a heating pad

- **Post-partum bleeding:** also known as lochia. This is like a heavy period and will last for up to six weeks after she has given birth (although it will get lighter). Make sure she has a plentiful supply of sanitary pads

MEDIC: STAND BY
Call your medical support team if your CO's bleeding becomes smelly or gets heavier, as this could indicate an infection.

- **Excessive sweating:** if your CO is at home, make sure that she has a plentiful supply of clean clothes, preferably cotton. Also change the sheets if she sweats heavily overnight

- **Increasing need to pee:** another way, along with sweating, of your CO's body ridding itself of excessive fluids. If it is very uncomfortable for her to pee, she might find it easier to take a pee in the bath. This will definitely reduce the sting. If she can't face that, an alternative is to fill a sports bottle full of cool water that she can squeeze onto her perineum while she pees. This will also ensure that the area is kept clean

- **Muscle strain and soreness:** your CO is probably going to ache all over. Running her a warm bath can help, as can massage
- **Stress incontinence:** your CO may find that as her pelvic floor regains its tone, she leaks urine. She may find this distressing, but it should be a temporary condition, typically a couple of months at most. When she is feeling stronger, there are pelvic exercises that she can do that will help with this problem
- **Headaches:** hormonal changes can trigger headaches. If you can support your CO to take moments to relax, such as in the bath or taking a nap, this may help reduce her stress and reduce the frequency of headaches
- **Breast pain:** your CO's first milk is colostrum, which is so nutrient-rich that she only has to produce relatively small amounts for your BT. However, three or four days after she has given birth, your CO will start producing regular breast milk, which your BT needs a lot more of. The process of switching between these two types of milk, and her breasts becoming engorged with breast milk, is referred to as her milk 'coming in'. Her breasts will be heavier and literally fuller. Your CO may find this process uncomfortable or even painful. If she is breastfeeding, this will provide some relief, as will a warm compress (a hot-water bottle or a heating pad). If she isn't breastfeeding, it can take up to 10 days for her body to get the message and stop producing milk. In the meantime she can find some relief by wearing a supportive bra. This shouldn't be too tight or it could increase her discomfort and also cause issues with blocked ducts and infection. A cold compress, such as a frozen bag of peas, will also help reduce the discomfort

MEDIC: STAND BY

Call your medical support team if your CO has pain in one of her breasts and also has flu-like symptoms (aches and pains and a high temperature) as she may have mastitis. This is painful inflammation of the breast tissue, which can be triggered by an infection.

COMMANDO DAD TOP TIP

Your CO's breasts are factories, not storage containers. In other words, they will regulate demand to meet supply. That is why it may not be a good idea to express milk to relieve engorgement – your CO's breasts will produce more milk and therefore exacerbate the problem. If she is breastfeeding, she may continue to produce more milk than your BT needs (although the excess can be frozen and may become useful if your CO wants to transition to bottle-feeding breast milk to your BT later). If your CO isn't breastfeeding, expressing may delay the process of her body ceasing to produce milk.

ADVICE FROM THE FRONT LINE

'You will need to do most things for your CO, who will likely be in a bit of pain and discomfort and not particularly mobile. Keeping the home tidy will help keep your mind ordered and reduce stress. Take time to prepare proper nutritionally balanced meals. My wife was pretty sleep deprived when she came back from hospital and I remember taking James in his carrycot into the living room while she slept. I also did all of the housework for the first couple of weeks.'

NEIL WHITE

VISITORS

It is to be expected that your friends and family will want to visit in those first few days and weeks – especially the new grandparents – but make sure you arrange a time that is at your convenience. You and your CO have a BT to look after, and she has just been through the physically draining experience of labour. Your primary concern must be maintaining as calm and relaxed an atmosphere at base camp as possible. You do not need the pressure of entertaining. You'll need to lay some ground rules, which may include visiting hours.

It is inevitable that some people may be a tad annoyed that they are not allowed immediate and continued access, but this will pass. You will thank yourself for it in the wee small hours, when you are administering a feed having had the benefit of a couple of hours' sleep that may otherwise have been spent entertaining.

ADVICE FROM THE FRONT LINE

'Don't let people tell you when they are coming round to meet your new BT. Tell them when is convenient for you and your routine. They will expect you to make cups of tea, as if you don't already have enough to do!'
MARK BAKER

That is not to say that visitors are always a bad thing. Visitors can offer practical help: picking up essential supplies on the way over or doing essential base camp admin while they are there: hanging out washing, washing up, helping to tidy up, cooking a meal etc. Your friends and family will want to offer practical help. Let them.

Be aware that visitors may want to give you the benefit of their experience of bringing up troopers. Remember that every BT is different and use the information that is offered – or not – as you see fit. Anyone who gets annoyed that you are not following your advice is not actually giving you advice, they're giving you orders. You do not have to take them.

ADVICE FROM THE FRONT LINE

'Do what works for you – every baby is different and no matter what parents/friends/in-laws tell you or suggest, only you will know what works for you and your BT. It is a steep learning curve and nothing will prepare you fully, especially the first time round. It is very much a case of trial and error and as long as BT is safe, well fed, clean and loved, just do what you feel is right – gut instinct has a large part to play.'

CALUM BEATT

COMMANDO DAD TOP TIP

Let people know beforehand your thoughts on visitors in the early weeks. If possible, schedule visits and ensure that people know that there's a set 'leaving time'. Do not feel guilty about turning unexpected visitors away. Your priority is your CO and BT.

FERTILITY

Be aware that your CO may be very fertile after giving birth. It is possible for her to get pregnant even if she is breastfeeding (which many believe limits fertility) and before she gets her first period after giving birth.

ADVICE FROM THE FRONT LINE

'As we left the hospital, our midwife told us that we needed to be careful as a woman is super fertile after giving birth. We both assured her that we were going to take a long rest from baby making. Exactly one year and two weeks later we welcomed our second son – Jude – into the world.'

NEIL SINCLAIR

RECAP AND REFRESH

Chapter 7: What happens next has provided you with information about:

- Holding your BT
- Feeding your BT
- Bringing your CO and BT back to base camp
- Your CO after birth
- Visitors at base camp

When things don't go to plan

8

THE BRIEF

We have established in this book that you need to be backup support to your CO. However, in some instances, you may both need backup support. Accept help when it is offered and ask for it when it is needed.

THE OBJECTIVE

By the end of this chapter you will have an overview of what to do, and where to ask for help, in a variety of situations. Do not read this to discover all the things that may go wrong – many things may go right. Worry is a negative emotion that achieves nothing. If you have any concerns about your CO's pregnancy, please discuss them now with your medical backup team – your midwife and doctor – as they are the medical experts who are there to help you.

The first aid information given in the 'Emergency deployment' section below has been approved by the British Red Cross Society. If you are reading outside the UK, you may also wish to check with your national Red Cross or Red Crescent society for information.

EMERGENCY DEPLOYMENT

An emergency deployment is when your BT arrives unexpectedly quickly, before you have time to get to the hospital or seek medical aid. Statistically, it is not likely your BT will deploy early, especially if this is your CO's first pregnancy. However, statistics aren't going to help you if your BT decides to put in a sudden appearance. Preparation and planning prevent poor parental performance, and so review this quick guide to what to do if an emergency deployment occurs.

 COMMANDO DAD TOP TIP
Remain calm and continue to reassure and encourage your CO throughout.

ADVICE FROM THE FRONT LINE

'The main advice I can give is to reassure your CO, try not to panic and keep a sense of humour about it all ... it's a natural event, but being on our own was a bit of a surprise.'
JON WHEALE, WHO DELIVERED HIS BT ON A PARK BENCH AT NIGHT

In the event of an emergency deployment, keep calm and follow these steps:

Call for help:
- Ring the emergency number on your CO's maternity notes or, if you can't find it, dial 999
- Give:
  - Your CO's name, address and phone number
  - How many weeks pregnant she is

- Any medical condition that your CO or BT may have
- Request immediate medical backup: a midwife and an ambulance
- They will stay on the line with you to help you through labour and, perhaps, delivery

If at base camp:
- Unlock the doors to allow access for medical backup
- If this occurs at night, turn on all the lights to guide the medical backup team to your base camp
- Collect items you'll need for the birth:
  - Clean sheets for your CO to give birth on
  - Clean towels and blankets to dry and cover your newborn BT
  - A large bowl, bucket or plastic bag for the placenta
- Help your CO strip from the waist down, put a sheet or blanket over her if she wants it
- Wash your hands
- Ensure the room you're in is warm and as draught-free as possible to help keep your BT and CO warm after deployment
- Ensure your CO is in as comfortable a position as possible

If out and about:
- You need to improvise, adapt and overcome
- When you call for medical backup, ensure they know you are not at base camp and provide as precise a set of details about your location as possible
- Ensure you are in the warmest, cleanest place available
- If you are in the car, use your 'Emergency deployment kit' if you were able to pack one beforehand. See the 'Planning and preparation prevent poor parental performance' section in *Chapter 6: Deployment day* for more information
- Help your CO strip from the waist down and find her something to cover herself with, if she wants it and there is something available
- Clean your hands – use hand sanitiser or sterile gloves (if you're in

the car, check your first aid kit, or emergency deployment kit)

- Find something that you can use to dry and warm your newborn BT, as clean as possible
- Ensure your CO is in as comfortable a position as possible

Preparing for delivery

- If contractions are rapid (two minutes apart or less) and your CO has an urge to push, but the medical backup team has not arrived, encourage her to try panting: three quick pants and a long blow can delay your BT's arrival for a few minutes
- If you can, encourage your CO to lie on her left side or to get on all fours with her bottom in the air and her head near the floor, as this too may ease the urge to push
- If your CO still has an overpowering urge to push – coupled with a feeling that she needs to have a bowel movement, which is actually your BT putting pressure on her rectum as they pass through the birth canal – you need to embrace the situation. Your BT is coming
- Whatever position your CO is in, position yourself to catch your BT. If she is on all fours as above, she needs to bring her bottom nearer the floor and you'll need to get behind her. If she is in a sitting up position – regardless of which way round – gravity will be on your side. Standing up is not advisable in case your BT is delivered very fast and falls
- Be aware that there is going to be a lot of blood and other fluids involved in the next stage

Delivery

- When your BT 'crowns' (i.e. you can see the head appear) encourage your CO to really push – to bear down as if she is on the loo
- Once the head is out, do not pull it
- Check that the umbilical cord isn't wrapped round their neck
  - If it is *loosely* round their neck, gently slip your fingers under the cord and ease it over their head

- If it is *tightly* round the neck, leave it as it could snap and cause complications. Your BT's body will be born with the next contraction and you can remove it from round their neck then
- Your BT's shoulders – the widest part of their body – need to be delivered next, one at a time. Your CO is advised to pant, not push, through this stage to prevent your BT being delivered too quickly and your CO tearing
- Your BT's head should gently rotate to one side to prepare for a shoulder to be delivered. If it doesn't, gently, and while still supporting your BT's head, gently guide the side of their head towards your CO's back. This should help a shoulder to be delivered with the next contraction
- The second shoulder will be delivered next and the rest of your BT will be delivered quickly after. Be prepared
- When your BT is deployed, leave the umbilical cord attached. The medical backup team will be able to see to this when they arrive
- Your BT may be born with a blue tinge to their skin – this is normal. They will also be wet with amniotic fluid, blood and coated in a white, waxy substance – vernix caseosa – which protected their skin during pregnancy. They will be slippery – be careful
- If your BT has good muscle tone (i.e. they're moving and active) and begins to cry, get them dry and warm immediately
- If your BT doesn't cry, is blue or grey and floppy, and you can't see their chest moving, then they're not breathing. If you are alone and the baby is not breathing, begin rescue breaths:

  1 Make sure that their airway is open. Put one finger on the point of the chin and lift it. Take care not to press on the soft part of the neck under the chin as that can block the airway
  2 Take a breath, then seal your lips tightly round your baby's mouth and nose. Blow gently until the baby's chest rises
  3 Remove your mouth and watch the chest fall back. A breath should take one second
  4 Repeat to give five rescue breaths

- You then need to begin chest compressions:
  1 Place the tips of two fingers on the centre of the baby's chest
  2 Press down firmly by one-third of the depth of the chest. Release the pressure but do not remove your fingers. Allow the chest to come back up fully. Repeat to give 30 compressions at a rate of 100–120 per minute
  3 Give your BT two rescue breaths into their mouth and nose
  4 Continue the cycle of 30 chest compressions to two rescue breaths for one minute. Remember, the ambulance should be on its way and the call handler will be able to guide you through these steps
  5 Continue giving CPR – 30 chest compressions followed by two rescue breaths – until emergency help arrives or your BT shows signs of regaining consciousness
- Get skin-on-skin contact with your BT and you or your CO as soon as possible (ensuring that your BT still has a blanket draped over them, especially their head). This will keep your new BT warm and help everyone calm down
- As the cord is still attached, your BT may need to rest on your CO's abdomen (as there may not be enough cord to allow them to be laid higher). However, if they can reach to her breasts, put them there to nuzzle as this will stimulate your CO to produce the hormone that will help her deliver the placenta

TOP TIP

COMMANDO DAD TOP TIP
If your CO gives birth to your BT outdoors, do not rub off the vernix caseosa as it can help keep your BT warm. Do pat your BT dry and get them against your CO's skin and under cover ASAP.

ADVICE FROM THE FRONT LINE

'I now know vernix (newborn cam cream?!) is waterproofing and prevents heat loss, so shouldn't be rubbed off, especially outside in the cold early hours of the morning.'
JON WHEALE

Delivering the placenta, or 'afterbirth'

- The placenta will be delivered after your BT's deployment – typically between 5 and 30 minutes
- If medical backup hasn't arrived and your CO feels the urge to push (much milder this time), encourage her to get into an upright position
- The placenta will normally be delivered in one or two contractions
- It will be bloody, warm and slippery, with the consistency of raw meat or liver
- Gently – as your BT is still attached to the placenta by the umbilical cord – put the placenta in a plastic bag or bucket next to your CO
- The medical support team will deal with the umbilical cord and the afterbirth when they arrive
- Vigorously rub your CO's abdomen, directly beneath her belly button, as this will help her uterus contract and keep any bleeding in check. If your CO can breastfeed, this will also help her uterus contract

TOP TIP **COMMANDO DAD TOP TIP**
Your BT and CO will be exhausted and cold after the birth. You have already ensured your BT is warm and dry and you must do the same for your CO. Where possible, remove all wet blankets, sheets and towels and replace with dry. Cover her with a warm blanket (make sure not to overheat your BT).

Breech delivery

Rarely a baby is born breech – i.e. feet or bottom first. You will probably know this is the case beforehand, due to ultrasounds, scans and midwife's checks. If this is the case:

- Follow the 'Call for help' steps, ensuring the medical backup support team knows your BT is breech
- Follow the 'Preparing for delivery' steps but, in addition, have your CO get on all fours
- During delivery, **do not touch** your BT until their head is out, as you may hamper the delivery and cause complications. This is because if you touch their body before they can see you, you may startle them and perhaps activate the 'Moro reflex', which will cause them to throw out their arms and gasp (while their head is still in amniotic fluid)
- Be prepared to catch your BT
- Follow the 'Delivering the placenta' steps

What not to do

There are some things that you *must* never do during an emergency birth:

- Do not panic. You need to keep clearheaded and help your CO remain as calm and focussed as possible
- Do not attempt to wipe away any fluid from your CO's vagina as you may contaminate her birth canal
- Do not pull your BT or exert pressure on them. Let them be born naturally
- Do not pull on the placenta – let it be delivered naturally
- Do not touch a breech BT until their head has been delivered
- Do not attempt to tie off or cut the placenta
- Do not give your CO medication

ADVICE FROM THE FRONT LINE

'After the penultimate contraction, Clementine's head was out ... I did instinctively pull and Emma (CO) said, loudly, not to ... Not panicking and waiting for the next contraction is essential.'
JON WHEALE

Backup support

When the medical support team arrives, make sure to tell them of any condition that your CO or BT may have, any medication your CO is taking and any allergies.

Following an emergency deployment, even where there were no complications, it is possible that your CO, and yourself, may feel traumatised. Do not waste time telling yourself you shouldn't be feeling this way – you are having a perfectly normal response to an experience that you found traumatic. A Commando Dad knows when to ask for and accept help – both for himself and his CO.

Places that can offer help include:

- Each other. You can reassure your CO that everything is OK and her feelings are normal, and vice versa
- Your midwife, who may be able to put you in contact with others who have been through the same experience, or know of local places that can provide support
- The National Childbirth Trust (NCT), who will also be able to put you in touch with others who have been through the same experience
- The Birth Trauma Association, a specialist charity that exists to provide support for people traumatised by childbirth: www.birthtraumaassociation.org.uk
- For more first aid information from the British Red Cross Society, visit redcross.org.uk/firstaid

ASSISTED DELIVERY

There may be instances where your CO may need help delivering your BT. This can be because:

- There are concerns that your BT is in distress and needs to be delivered quickly
- Your BT is in an awkward position and so is not moving out of the birth canal as would normally be expected. They may need to be turned
- Your CO is exhausted and/or is unable to push

In these instances, a ventouse (vacuum extractor) or forceps can be used. Your midwife or doctor will decide which instrument would be the most appropriate, based on your CO and BT's situation. Both are safe, but may cause additional tissue damage to the perineum. In the event of an assisted delivery:

- Your midwife or doctor will explain the procedure to your CO and seek her verbal permission
- Your CO will have her bladder emptied via a catheter (a tube inserted directly into her bladder). The catheter may need to remain in after the delivery
- If your CO hasn't had an epidural, she will need a local anaesthetic in her perineum
- Your midwife or doctor may need to perform an episiotomy (i.e. cut your CO's perineum) to help your BT be delivered, which is more likely if forceps are being used
- Your doctor or midwife will have decided on the most effective instrument:
  - **Ventouse**, which uses suction to attach a cup onto your BT's head. Once attached, they will wait until your CO is having a contraction and advise her to push, while they gently pull to help deliver your BT. It may take more than one contraction
  - **Forceps:** which are like long, smooth metal salad spoons, curved to fit around a BT's head. They will wait until your CO is having a

contraction and advise her to push, while they gently pull to help deliver your BT. It may take more than one contraction

- When your BT is delivered, they may have bruising, swelling, a slightly elongated head, marks or small cuts, but these are temporary. Your BT will be checked over by a doctor or nurse specialising in newborns directly after their delivery
- Your CO may have to have some aftercare if she has an assisted delivery as it may increase her risk of developing blood clots. This may include wearing surgical stockings or having daily injections of heparin. Your midwife or doctor will advise you both if this is the case

Occasionally, if a ventouse has been used but didn't work, the midwife or doctor may then attempt to use forceps. If neither work, and there are concerns about the wellbeing of your BT or CO, it may be necessary for your CO to be taken for an emergency Caesarean section.

CAESAREAN SECTION (C-SECTION)

A Caesarean is an operation to deliver your BT in which a doctor makes a cut in your CO's abdomen and uterus.

In some circumstances – such as your CO expecting twins or multiples or your midwife or doctor believing a vaginal delivery might be dangerous for your CO or BT – your CO can choose to have a Caesarean. This is called a planned, or elective, Caesarean.

An emergency Caesarean is where there are complications or difficulties during labour that mean your BT needs to be delivered urgently. It is an operation and will need to take place in an operating theatre. In the event of an emergency Caesarean:

- Stay calm. This is a stressful, fast-moving situation and you need to reassure your CO that she is in safe hands. You will be given surgical attire (gown, facemask etc) to wear
- Your midwife or doctor will explain the procedure to your CO and seek her permission. It may not be possible for your CO to sign a

consent form, so this may be verbal consent

- Your CO will have a drip inserted into a vein in her hand or arm to deliver fluids and medicines. She will also need to have her bladder emptied via a catheter (a tube inserted directly into her bladder). The catheter may need to remain in after the delivery
- If your CO has an epidural inserted already, she may have it topped up. If she has not, then she may be given a 'spinal' – an injection of drugs directly into the sac of fluid that surrounds her spinal cord. This will have the same painkilling power as an epidural, and is very fast-acting (your CO will feel the benefit within minutes)
- Your CO's abdomen will be cleaned with an antiseptic and there will be a screen put up so that she can't see what's being done
- Your CO may not be able to feel pain, but she will experience the sensation of deep pulling. She will also be able to hear everything
- Your BT will be delivered within ten minutes and once they have been checked over, they will be handed to your CO
- The surgeon will then remove the placenta and stitch up the wound. On the outer part of the wound they will use stitches or staples that will need to be removed when the wound is fully healed
- An uncomplicated Caesarean will be completed within an hour
- Your CO will need to stay in hospital for two or three days and there will be aftercare needed. This may include moving around as soon as possible, wearing surgical stockings or having daily injections of heparin to prevent blood clots. Your midwife will also provide your CO with advice on cleaning her wound to prevent infection and post-natal exercises

In a small number of cases, it may be necessary for your CO to have a Caesarean under general anaesthetic. In these instances, you will not be allowed to stay with her during the delivery.

ADVICE FROM THE FRONT LINE

'The C-section was rough. I was not allowed in until everything had been set up and I sat behind the screen as they did their work ... I felt helpless, but had to stay strong for her. Although she could feel no pain, she felt every tug.'

PAUL DRAKE

MEDIC: STAND BY

Call the medical support team if your CO experiences any of these problems after a Caesarean, as they may indicate an infection or blood clot: severe pain, leaking urine, painful or excessive vaginal bleeding, a cough or shortness of breath, swelling or pain in her calf.

IF YOUR BT NEEDS SPECIAL CARE

If your BT is born prematurely, is underweight, suffering from illness or experienced complications during birth, then they may need to spend some time in the Special Care Baby Unit (SCBU) or a neonatal intensive care unit (NICU).

These special units are designed to provide your BT with constant, specialised care and although it can make you feel helpless to see them dependent on machines and medication, rest assured that they are getting the help they need to build their strength and stay well.

In the case of premature BTs, the priority is to provide the care that they otherwise would have received inside your CO's body: help with breathing, feeding and warmth. This means that your BT may:

- Have tubes in their nose or mouth to help them breathe, until they can breathe on their own

- Have wires connected to their bodies, to monitor their heart and breathing
- Need to have a feeding tube, which delivers milk straight into their stomach

If your BT is thought to be weak, susceptible to illness, or already suffering from an infection or ailment, they may be isolated and kept in an incubator.

If your BT requires uncomfortable treatments, such as injections and blood tests, or if they have intense pain through a condition or an operation, they will receive painkillers in these units. Your doctor or midwife will be able to talk you through any side effects. They will also be able to advise you about how much physical contact you can have with your BT. Skin-on-skin contact with your BT and your CO can soothe you all.

IF YOUR CO DEVELOPS POST-NATAL DEPRESSION

It is hardly surprising after the physical and emotional experience of pregnancy and childbirth, your CO may feel down for a few days afterwards. This may manifest itself as:

- Crying
- Feeling anxious
- Difficulty sleeping

This mild depression is known as 'baby blues' and can be caused by:

- Fluctuating hormone levels. After birth, pregnancy hormones bottom out while others, such as those required to produce milk, rise rapidly. She is on a hormonal rollercoaster
- Extreme tiredness. Your CO will be very tired after labour and then will enter into the sleep-deprived existence that is early parenthood
- Anxiety caused by having a new BT to look after, or difficulty with mastering skills, such as breastfeeding

This may last for a few days and then disappear. During the time that your CO is suffering with baby blues, be supportive. Allow her to cry as this is a physical and emotional release. As a Commando Dad, you will be tactful and empathetic.

However, if the blues last longer than a couple of weeks, it may be an indicator for post-natal depression. This is an illness that requires treatment. The good news is that every CO recovers and returns to her 'old self'. The bad news is that many COs do not recognise the symptoms of post-natal depression or are afraid to admit their negative feelings. This will delay them visiting the doctor and getting the help they need.

Symptoms include, but are not limited to:
- Persistent negative emotions: anxiety, fear, guilt, sadness or hopelessness
- Physical manifestations of anxiety: racing heart, sweating, panic attacks
- Crying and irritability
- Changes in appetite
- Taking no pleasure from being with your BT or feeling hostile towards them, or you
- Exhaustion and lacking in motivation to do anything

How you can help:
- Recognise that this is an illness; she can't help the way she feels. She needs to see a doctor. Go together
- Listen to her thoughts and fears and be supportive and sympathetic. Reassure her that she will get better
- Try to provide her with time to relax without your BT, and also get a break from the household chores. Discuss this beforehand so that she doesn't feel that you have taken over because she is a bad or incapable parent or not coping. Interpreting your help in this way is a manifestation of her illness

Further advice and support:
- National Childbirth Trust (NCT): www.nct.org.uk
- The Association for Post-Natal Illness (APNI): www.apni.org
- Pre and Postnatal Depression Advice and Support (PANDAS): www.pandasfoundation.org.uk

IF YOUR BABY DIES

It is a sad fact that every day in the UK, 17 babies die before, during or shortly after birth. That is around 6,500 babies each year. This does not include the numbers of late miscarriages and babies who are born dead before 24 completed weeks of pregnancy. The death of a baby is a major bereavement and the stage that the pregnancy had reached does not predict the length or the depth of the grief that the parents experience.

I am so sorry if this has happened to you. Throughout this book, I have focussed on you providing backup support to your partner, but if your baby dies before, during or shortly after birth, you both need help and support. Please do not feel as if you have to cope alone. You don't. This section covers some of the information you will need and suggests other sources of information and support.

Your CO may require surgical or medical support. Your midwife and doctor will be able to provide you with more information, based on your specific set of circumstances. There will be decisions to take. If these are about the care your CO needs, either before, during or after the birth, legally these decisions are hers. After the birth, decisions about the baby should be made jointly, but don't feel you need to hurry through them. Most decisions can wait.

While she is in hospital, your CO and you should be cared for in a quiet room where you can't hear other parents and babies and where you can stay together after the birth. You should also be able to spend time with your baby if you want to, and to create mementoes such as photographs and hand and foot prints. The staff will suggest what you can do and it is up to the two of you to decide what you want.

Many parents find these physical reminders of their baby invaluable in the weeks, months and years to come. So even if you are unsure, you might say yes, for example, to having photographs, which can either be stored in your CO's hospital record or given to you in a plain envelope in case you change your mind in the future. You will find more about creating memories in the Sands booklet *Saying Goodbye to Your Baby,* which is available as a download on their website www.uk-sands.org.

Some hospitals will have specially trained bereavement midwives who can provide you with the specialist support you need. Sands, the stillbirth and neonatal death charity, supports parents of babies who die before, during or after birth. They will not only be able to offer you and your partner straightforward guidance on the practical steps that you need to take, but also emotional support in the times ahead.

If your baby was born dead after 24 completed weeks of pregnancy, this is defined in law as a stillbirth, which must be registered. If your baby was born alive and then died, the birth and death must also be registered. Your baby's name can be included in the register and on the certificate you will be offered, but names cannot be added later or changed. So it is important to decide what you want to call your baby before going to the register office. The hospital team will give you information about how to register.

Stillborn babies and babies who were born alive and then died must, by law, have a funeral. The team at the hospital will be able to tell you what needs to be done and what your options are. This information is also available on the Sands website.

If your baby died between 14 and 24 weeks, the hospital may refer to your baby as a late miscarriage. This is not intended to undermine your feelings of grief or cause you distress. This term is used because 24 weeks is the legal age of viability: that is, the point at which a baby is thought to stand a good chance of survival if born. If your baby died prior to 24 weeks, there will be no birth or death certificate. But that does not mean you will have nothing to remember your baby by. You can still have a funeral. The hospital should also offer you a hospital certificate to keep, on which you can enter your baby's name and other details.

If your baby died prior to 14 weeks, it is referred to as a miscarriage. Miscarriages are most common in this stage of the pregnancy, which is one of the reasons that the initial booking appointment with your antenatal team happens beyond this point. Again, that is not to dismiss your feelings of grief or the impact of the bereavement. There may not be any physical remains of your baby, but you can still mark your loss. The Miscarriage Association, the charity for those affected by the loss of a baby in pregnancy, will be able to provide advice, information and support.

 ADVICE FROM THE FRONT LINE

'Our BT was our third attempt at getting pregnant after two miscarriages. I don't think anything can prepare you for the change in emotion after that. We were in bits. My advice for other dads would be: don't be afraid to talk! Whether it's to a good friend or your other half. It's no good bottling it up and being all macho. We have feelings! You have both suffered a loss.'
DAVE BOATWRIGHT

There is no right or wrong way to be feeling. The charities mentioned here may be able to help you understand the emotions that you're going through, and how grief manifests itself, physically and emotionally.

If you and your partner were expecting twins or multiple babies
If you and your partner were expecting twins or multiple babies and lost one or more of your babies, TAMBA, the Twins & Multiple Births Association, has a support group that can help. They can provide

support, information, understanding and a unique insight into the complex emotions around losing one or more of your babies.

If you lost your baby through an ectopic pregnancy

If you have lost your baby through an ectopic pregnancy, The Ectopic Pregnancy Trust can provide help and support. They have insight into the issues surrounding ectopic pregnancy – which, depending on the time it was discovered, could involve life-saving surgery – and provide services to help you deal with the impact.

More information

There are people out there who have been through the same experience and can listen and offer you support:

- Sands has created a booklet specifically for dads, called *Mainly for Fathers*. It is available as a free download from the Sands website and will provide information that will be useful to both you and your partner, but which has been tailored for you: www.uk-sands.org. Sands also offer other practical booklets and support over the phone, online (email and forum) and in a hundred local support groups across the UK. Many of the Sands staff who provide this support are also bereaved parents.
- The Miscarriage Association provides a helpline, online (email and forum) support and local support groups across the UK: www.miscarriageassociation.org.uk
- TAMBA Bereavement Support Group, part of TAMBA, the Twins & Multiple Births Association, can provide support if you have lost one or more babies from a multiple birth. They offer a befriending service, where a parent who has lost one or more babies from a multiple birth will be able to offer support, parent to parent. There's also online support via a Facebook page. TAMBA BSG has also created a booklet that includes a section for dads: *For Parents Who Have Lost One or More Babies from a Multiple Birth*. It is available as a free download from their website

- The Ectopic Pregnancy Trust provides information and support via a telephone helpline and an online forum: www.ectopic.org.uk.

RECAP AND REFRESH

Chapter 8, When things don't go to plan has provided you with information about:
- Emergency deployment
- Assisted delivery
- Caesarean section
- Special care your BT may need
- Post-natal depression: signs and symptoms
- If your baby dies

By being prepared beforehand about things that *may* not go to plan, you will be forearmed. In the event that the delivery doesn't go to plan or your CO develops post-natal depression, stay calm and support your CO. Help is available. Know when to ask for – and accept – it.

In the event that your baby dies during your CO's pregnancy, or shortly after birth, you will both need help and support. As bereaved parents you do not need to cope alone.

Special ops:

When your experience is different from the norm

9

THE BRIEF
No two parenting missions are the same, but by and large the majority of them do share certain characteristics: they are conducted by parents in a committed relationship and they give birth to a single BT in a hospital. However, this by no means represents the story for all parents. Some parents are on special ops – that is, their experience is a little special, or different from the norm.

THE OBJECTIVE
By the end of this chapter you will have information to support you and your CO if you plan to go on special ops, that is, if you are expecting multiple deployments; are considering giving birth outside a hospital setting or having a medication-free birth; or are using a surrogate. There's also a section for young dads.

MULTIPLE DEPLOYMENTS

If your CO is expecting more than one BT, a lot of the advice in this book is still relevant to you. She will still need to eat well, take care of herself and have your full backup support. However, there will be some differences, which are outlined below. It is important to remember that, just because twin and multiple pregnancies are considered higher risk, does not mean that your CO will have problems. But she will need to be monitored more closely.

Ultrasound scans

- Your CO will have more scans than the usual two, usually every four weeks until 32 weeks, then fortnightly until birth. The frequency of scans will depend on the hospital and clinical need
- The first ultrasound scan (8–14 weeks) will confirm whether your CO is expecting twins or multiples. The scan will confirm:
  - Whether your BTs are in the same amniotic sac. If the amniotic sac is shared, they will certainly be identical. If they have separate amniotic sacs, they may still be identical, but it is less likely
  - Whether your BTs share a placenta. If they do, your medical support team will want to scan your BTs regularly to make sure they're both getting the nutrition they need
- The 'anomaly scan' – all COs have this around 18–22 weeks – will confirm whether your BTs are developing normally
- Additional scans will be available to your CO to check on your BTs' growth and positioning
- At 34 weeks, if your CO is expecting twins, the position of the leading baby will be checked to determine the best method for delivery
- As with any pregnancy, tests for other rare conditions may be offered where there is a family history

Routine blood tests

Routine blood tests remain the same as in any pregnancy unless there is a medical problem.

Diagnostic tests

If your CO opts to have screening for Down's syndrome, then the nuchal translucency scan measurements will be taken to assess your BTs' chances of having Down's syndrome. If a high probability is found, your CO will be offered a diagnostic test that can determine more accurately whether each baby has the syndrome. Discuss these tests with your midwife for an overview of any risks so that you and your CO can make a judgement about what works for you.

Antenatal care

Your CO should receive more than the standard seven to ten antenatal appointments so that the progress of your BTs can be monitored very closely. This is especially the case if your BTs were conceived as a result of IVF treatment.

Find out if your local hospital has the following things:

- Arrangements for antenatal care in multiple pregnancies. This could be a midwife, doctor or consultant who specialises in multiple births
- A procedure for multiple births
- A midwife who specialises in breastfeeding support for twins and multiples

Delivery

Below are some observations about delivering twins and multiples. Remember, your CO may not be typical and none of these may apply to you. But to be forewarned is forearmed:

- Twins and multiples are typically born earlier than single BTs
- Whether your BTs will be born vaginally or by Caesarean section will be determined by how they are positioned or 'presenting' in your CO's uterus. Ideally, BTs need to be positioned head down for

a vaginal birth

- Your CO is more likely to be encouraged to have an epidural, not because labour with twins or multiples is more painful, but because it is more likely that your CO will need to have a Caesarean
- Your CO's delivery will not necessarily be longer or more difficult than a typical delivery
- If your BTs are born prematurely or if there are complications, they may need to spend some time in the Special Care Baby Unit (SCBU).
- The SCBU can provide the care that your BTs would have received inside your CO's body and help with breathing, feeding and warmth. Your BTs may:
  - Have tubes in their noses or mouths to help them breathe, until they can breathe on their own
  - Have wires connected to their bodies, to monitor their hearts and breathing
  - Need to have a feeding tube, which delivers milk straight into their stomach
  - Need to spend time in an incubator

TOP TIP

COMMANDO DAD TOP TIP
    As multiple deployments typically happen early, you're going to need to book antenatal classes sooner rather than later. With twins, classes should ideally be completed by the 34th week of pregnancy; for triplets, by the 30th week. TAMBA (Twins & Multiple Births Association) offer antenatal classes solely for parents of twins and multiple BTs throughout the UK: www.tamba.org.uk.

Breastfeeding

Managing twin and multiple feeding can be a challenge. The mechanics are the same, but the logistics are different.

Your CO should be able to produce enough milk as breastfeeding works on the principle of supply and demand – the more your BTs feed, the more milk will be produced. But your BTs will need to suck effectively to stimulate this production.

As twins and multiples are typically born earlier, they are often small and sleepy, making it more difficult to suck effectively. If your CO chooses to breastfeed but comes up against this issue, she may wish to express breast milk. In this instance, you will be able to feed your BTs via a feeding tube or bottle.

Backup support

Your CO alone needs to do all the physical work to produce your BTs. A lot of common complaints associated with pregnancy – for example, morning sickness and fatigue – are a result of soaring pregnancy hormones. Your CO has even higher hormone levels than a woman expecting a single BT and so she may experience symptoms more acutely. You may be called upon to offer physical support, such as taking care of your CO and doing extra chores around the house, quite early in the pregnancy.

Your CO may also feel anxious at the thought of delivering your BTs or being able to cope with the reality of everyday life with multiple BTs to care for. Encourage her to share these feelings with you or her medical support team. Both of you need to find out as much as possible about twins and multiple births. TAMBA, The Twins & Multiple Births Association, provides downloadable booklets via their site and information about antenatal classes. There's also a confidential support line for both of you, should you need it: www.tamba.org.uk Helpline: 0800 138 0509.

HOME BIRTH

Throughout this book, I have referred to your CO delivering at a hospital. However, she may decide to deliver at home – i.e base camp. If your CO is considered to have a low-risk pregnancy, i.e. she has had no complications throughout her pregnancy, is carrying a single BT and has no serious medical history, then there is no reason why home birth shouldn't be an option.

If you and your CO are considering a home birth, you can discuss it with your midwife, who can provide guidance and help you make an informed decision based on your personal circumstances and whether support for this type of birth is available in your area.

If you do decide to have a home birth, your midwife can provide antenatal care tailored to a home birth and advise you how to book it.

COMMANDO DAD TOP TIP

TOP TIP

Your CO may put a home birth in her birth plan, but then change her mind. This will cause no issues and she is free to change her mind at any time prior to the late stages of labour. For this reason, it is best for you to know the route to the local hospital, just in case.

Pros

If your CO does decide to deliver at home, there are a number of advantages:

- As your CO is in her home environment, she is likely to be more relaxed than she would be in hospital
- It removes the anxiety of knowing the right time to decamp to the hospital for delivery and you won't have to leave afterwards
- It is easier for you and your CO to control the environment than it is in hospital:
  - Your CO can move through your home and will not be confined to a single birthing suite. She will only periodically be checked over (rather than constantly, as she would be in hospital)
  - Your CO can eat and drink as she chooses
  - She has more freedom to choose the room she delivers in (there may be some restrictions depending on your home) and the position
  - You can dim the lights and create a more 'low-key' environment than may be possible in your hospital's birthing suite

- You are more likely to be assisted in the birth by the midwife who your CO has built a relationship with over the pregnancy. In hospital, you will be assisted by the midwife on duty and, although of course they have equal levels of specialist training to your own midwife, neither of you will be familiar with them. At a home birth, you will have two midwives to assist your CO – one for her and one to look after your BT.

Cons

There are some disadvantages of a home birth that you will need to consider:

- Your CO's pain relief options will be limited. The epidural is not available in a home setting, for example, but gas and air is
- If you need emergency assistance, your CO will need to be transferred to the hospital. Caesarean section and forceps deliveries are not available in a home setting, for example
- If your newborn BT requires medical attention, they will need to be transferred to the hospital.
- Any 'mess' associated with childbirth will be in your own home. However, cleaning up afterwards will be straightforward: your midwife will bring coverings to protect your home and will clear up the placenta and the afterbirth
- After labour and childbirth, you will both immediately be responsible for looking after your new BT. In hospital you will have the physical and emotional support and care of the hospital staff. They can provide food, practical advice such as how to change a nappy and medical assistance and information

TOP TIP **COMMANDO DAD TOP TIP**
If you're using a birthing pool, make sure you have a thermometer and leave enough time to fill it up. It will take approximately an hour using a kitchen tap.

ADVICE FROM THE FRONT LINE

'My son was born at home and it was a great experience, really intimate and personal, but also surreal. It was scary while we waited for the midwives to arrive because contractions got closer and my wife said she wanted to push. When the midwives arrived, I wasn't just there comforting and holding my wife's hand, I was actively involved in the birth and getting things ready. After my son was born, I sat and cuddled him on our sofa, which was fantastic. My wife could relax at home – there was no changing on to a ward. The midwives were great and it was really comfortable.'

MARC TOPLISS, whose first BT was born in hospital and his second at base camp

BIRTH AT A MIDWIFE-LED UNIT

A midwife-led unit is a small maternity unit based alongside, or near, a local hospital. They are staffed by midwives and aim to provide a relaxed, home-from-home environment for you and your CO. It provides an alternative if your CO is not comfortable with a home birth, but would prefer not to give birth in a hospital. If your CO is considered to be 'low risk', then this could be an option to consider.

You and your CO will need to check if one of these units is available in your area or within what you consider to be reasonable travelling distance. They are known by a variety of terms, including:

- Birth centre
- Maternity home or unit
- Community maternity unit

Pros

If your CO does decide to deliver in a midwife-led unit, there are a number of advantages:

- These are specialised units that exist only to support pregnant and labouring women
- They are designed to be like a home from home. Facilities may include a kitchen and lounge area, and TV and music facilities. Check what is available in your local unit
- Similar to a home birth, it is easier for you and your CO to control the environment than it is in hospital
  - Your CO will have greater freedom of movement as she will not be attached to a machine to check your BT. Your BT will be checked routinely via Doppler and palpation
  - Your CO can eat and drink as she chooses
  - It may be possible to dim the lights and create a more 'low-key' environment than in your hospital's birthing suite
- It is possible that you and your CO could meet all the staff at the unit prior to her going into labour, meaning that your CO will be assisted by someone she is familiar with
- After labour and childbirth, you will have the physical and emotional support and care of the midwives
- You may be able to stay at the maternity unit with your CO and BT overnight
- The midwife unit will be well stocked with labour aids, such as birthing pools and birthing balls
- The midwife-led unit may also provide supplementary services for your CO while she is pregnant. These could include reflexology, water birth workshops, antenatal and post-natal classes. Check what is available in your local unit

Cons

There are some disadvantages of your CO giving birth in a midwife-led unit that you will need to consider:

- Your CO's pain relief options will be limited. The epidural is not available in a midwife-led unit for example, but gas and air is
- If you need emergency assistance, your CO will need to be transferred to the hospital. Caesarean sections are not available in a midwife-led unit, but forceps may be
- If your newborn BT requires medical attention, they will be transferred to the hospital

TOP TIP

COMMANDO DAD TOP TIP

As with a hospital birth, you will need to factor in the time it takes to get to the unit when working out when to leave home.

NATURAL CHILDBIRTH

Natural childbirth is a term used to describe a medication-free birth. This can happen in any place that your CO decides to give birth: in a hospital, a midwife-led centre or at home. However, if your CO gives birth in hospital, you will need to be her advocate and make sure the staff on duty know her wishes.

Natural childbirth is ultimately your CO's decision and she will be able to discuss it with her midwife, who can help her make a judgement based on your individual circumstances.

Pros

If your CO does decide on a natural childbirth, there are a number of advantages:

- Certain pain medications, such as epidurals, can actually slow down labour. So labour is likely to be quicker without them
- Your CO will have more freedom of movement (including trying a number of different positions for birth) than she would if she were medicated
- Your CO will remain alert throughout labour and delivery and may be able to take a more active role than would be possible if she were medicated

- After birth, your CO will not have to overcome any lingering effects of medication
- There is no issue of medication crossing the placenta and affecting your BT

Cons

There are some disadvantages of your CO having a natural birth that you will need to consider:

- Natural methods of managing pain during labour do just that: manage it. They do not eliminate it. It may be very difficult for you to see your CO in pain
- Without pain relief, your CO may get very tired. This may impact her ability to push
- If complications arise, your CO may need medical intervention. This may lead to feelings of disappointment. You will need to reassure her

COMMANDO DADS WHO USE A SURROGATE

If you are a Commando Dad who is using a surrogate – either because you and your CO were unable to conceive or because you are part of a gay couple – congratulations on reaching this point. You have negotiated your way through a complex legal process, your relationship has withstood the necessary scrutiny, artificial insemination has been successful and you have found a suitable surrogate to carry your BT.

Depending on your wishes and the arrangements that you have with your surrogate, you and your partner may be able to be closely involved in the pregnancy and even present at the birth.

As you will be aware, at birth your surrogate is the legal mother of your BT, even if your BT is not genetically related to her. If she is married or in a civil partnership, her husband or partner will be regarded as the legal father. If she is unmarried, then the biological father can be named on the birth certificate.

The next stage is for you and your partner to become the legal parents of your BT, through a parental order or adoption:

- A parental order confers full parental status to you and your partner and requires that your BT is genetically related to one or both of you. Applications must be made to the court within six months of the birth of your BT. You and your partner must be husband and wife, civil partners or two persons who are living as partners
- Where you and your partner are not genetically related to your BT, you will need to go through the adoption process. Therefore, you will need to include a registered adoption agency in the surrogacy process

Unfortunately, you are not legally entitled to take leave from work to spend time at home with your new BT. However, your employer may offer this type of leave as part of its benefits package or be willing to discuss special arrangements. Check with your HR department.

More information:

Surrogacy UK is a not-for-profit organisation that can provide advice, support and information, whatever stage you are at in your surrogate journey: www.surrogacyuk.org.

YOUNG COMMANDO DADS (AGED 16–24)

Becoming a Commando Dad at a young age can present a specific set of complex issues, but these are not insurmountable. Your age alone does not make you a 'bad' dad, any more than every older dad is a 'good' one. But you may find that you experience a lack of support, or you are not included by, many of the services that exist to support parents.

The good news is that there is help and support out there for you if you need it, but you're going to need to take the initiative and seek it out yourself.

Gentlemen, it's probably not going to be easy, but nothing worth doing ever is.

ADVICE FROM THE FRONT LINE

'Becoming a parent is both exciting and rewarding whatever your age; I had no idea what to expect when my first son was born, but was surprised at how satisfying being a parent could be. Inevitably, life changes beyond recognition once the new baby arrives and being a young dad I was ready to meet the challenge head on and embrace the change. I am now the father of two boys and as a stay-at-home dad I've been able to spend more time with them than the average working dad probably would. I've been there at each developmental milestone and have been fascinated to see the way they have grown into little people. Experiencing parenthood at 23, I have had the energy to give my children lots of stimulating play and activities, something I may have lacked as an older dad. Being a dad isn't always easy, but it is the most important job you can ever do.'

JAMES HEYWOOD

Below I have listed some typical issues that young dads face. However, you may not be a typical young dad, and these may not necessarily apply to you. Similarly, I may not have touched on issues that you are experiencing. See the links under 'More information' for further help and support:

- **Attitudes:** unfortunately, for some people 'young' is synonymous with 'irresponsible'. Be aware of their negative perceptions, but do not accept them. Keep calm and show your maturity through your words and actions

- **Not feeling capable enough to be a dad:** the vast majority of Commando Dads spend time doubting their abilities to be capable dads. We all worry that we might not be able to handle the practicalities of looking after a BT, while at the same time shouldering the awesome responsibility of becoming the most important man in the world to a tiny new life. This is a perfectly understandable reaction to impending fatherhood. However, there is a difference between *thinking* you're not capable and actually *being* incapable. There are antenatal and parenting courses available to teach you the skills you need to take care of your BT: the only thing you cannot physically do is breastfeed

- **Maintaining relationships:**
  - **With the mother of your BT:** finding out you're expecting a BT does not necessarily mean that your relationship will end, but evidence would suggest that many young dads do find themselves in this situation. If this is the case for you, recognise that there is a difference between *parenting* and being in a relationship. In other words, although it obviously makes sense to be on friendly terms with the mother of your BT if possible, you do not need to be in a (romantic) relationship with her in order to share the parenting responsibilities of your BT

  - **With your parents, and the parents of your BT's mother:** even the most supportive families may be challenged by the news that you are going to become a parent. However, maintaining good relationships with your own family where possible is strongly advised, as they can provide help, support and love to you and your BT. If you or your partner are still living at home, then both sets of parents (now grandparents) are likely to play a major role in providing and caring for your BT

  - **With the professionals who are supporting your BT's mother:** where possible, engage with midwives, health visitors, social workers or the staff of children's centres. They can provide you with information and support, which may help you build confidence in your ability to support your BT and their mother

- Friends: you may feel as if you have less in common with your friends now that you are going to be a dad, and it is certainly true that they may not be able to understand your circumstances. However, don't cut all ties with your friends as this may leave you feeling isolated
- **Building new relationships:**
  - **Other new dads:** it can be very helpful to meet other young dads who can appreciate your experience first-hand. To find what's available in your area, go to the Dads' Map on YoungDads.tv (contact details below)
  - **Professional support services for new dads:** there are specialist information services available for you that can appreciate the multiple and complex needs of being a young dad. They can also provide advice on the practical and financial help and support that are available to you, as well as putting you in touch with other young dads
- **Know your rights:** if you and the mother of your BT don't stay together, find out how to apply to have contact with your child and whether you are expected to pay maintenance by contacting your local Citizens Advice Bureau

More information

- Young Dads TV: www.youngdads.tv
- Citizens Advice Bureau: www.citizensadvice.org.uk
- Barnardo's Babyfather Initiative: http://www.barnardos.org.uk/babyfather.htm
- Working with Men (WWM): www.workingwithmen.org

RECAP AND REFRESH

Chapter 9: Special ops: when your experience is a little different from the norm provided you with information about:

- Multiple deployments: if you and your CO are expecting twins or multiples
- Breastfeeding
- Home birth
- Birth at a midwife-led unit
- Natural childbirth
- Commando Dads who use a surrogate
- Young Commando Dads

Mission debrief

CONGRATULATIONS, GENTLEMEN.
Phase one of your fatherhood mission is now complete — you have proved effective backup support to your CO and paved the way for your new baby trooper. It's now time to put down *Commando Dad: Raw Recruits*, pick up your baby trooper and begin the next phase of your fatherhood adventure.

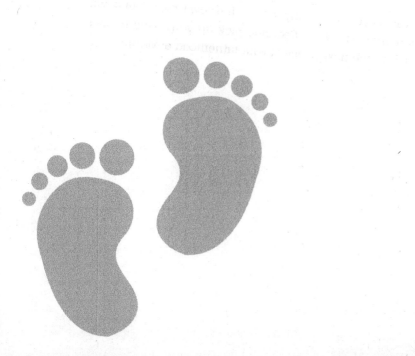

This is a precious – and short-lived – time. In fewer than 2,000 days the trooper in your arms will be five and beginning school; in fewer than 7,000 they will be 18. In order to make every second you spend together count, you need to apply military precision to your parenting: get organised, get the trooper admin squared away and be hands on from Day 1. Act in a way befitting your Commando Dad status.

You owe it to yourself – and your trooper – to be the best dad you can be. Right now.

GOOD LUCK GENTLEMEN.

ADVICE FROM THE FRONT LINE

'My advice is what you don't know, you will figure out, and what you think you can't cope with, you will. What parts of it will you enjoy? Not all of them, but the bits that you do, you will remember for ever.'
JAMES FENWICK

Glossary: breaking the code

THE BRIEF
Medical terminology can sometimes be overwhelming, especially when abbreviated in maternity notes. You need to decrypt the code.

THE OBJECTIVE
By the end of this chapter you will have a greater under-standing of common words, terms and abbreviations that you may come across over the next nine months. Abbreviations indicate how this term may appear in maternity notes. If you have any questions or concerns, please discuss them with your midwife or doctor, they are there to help you.

If there's a term not included here, please share it with me – and other dads – on the Commando Dad forums: www.commandodad.com/forum/. I will ensure it is added to the *Resources* section of the Commando Dad website and future editions of the book.

A

Active labour: when labour really gets going: your CO's cervix dilates (opens) more rapidly and contractions are closer together.

AFP – Alpha-fetoprotein: a protein found in the blood, measured during antenatal screening.

Afterbirth: the name given to the placenta when you CO delivers it after the birth of your BT. The part of labour when the placenta is delivered is called the third stage of labour.

ALB – Albumin: a protein. Your CO's urine will be tested for albumin, as it can be a sign of pre-eclampsia (a type of high blood pressure in pregnancy)

Amniocentesis: an antenatal test. A small sample of amniotic fluid is drawn out of your CO's uterus using a long hollow needle. The fluid is then tested for indicators of abnormalities.

Amniotic fluid: the liquid that surrounds and protects your BT and aids in their growth. It is mainly water, but from week 10 onwards your BT passes tiny amounts of urine into the fluid. It is the 'water' that is released when your CO's waters break.

Antenatal: before the birth of your BT. Sometimes called prenatal or antepartum.

Antenatal depression: a rarer, but equally as debilitating condition as post-natal depression. Seek support from your medical backup team.

Antenatal steroids: steroids given to help your BT's lungs and other organs mature more rapidly when it is expected they will be delivered preterm (before 36 weeks).

Antepartum: before the birth of your BT. Sometimes called prenatal or antenatal.

Anterior position: the preferred position for birth, when your BT is head down with the back of their head positioned slightly toward your CO's tummy. BTs tend to assume this position toward the end of pregnancy.

APGAR score/test: the APGAR test will be carried out one minute after your BT is born, and again at five minutes, for a quick evaluation of their physical health. Appearance, Pulse, Grimace (response to stimulation), Activity and Respiration are measured. Your BT will be given a mark out of 10, and a score between 7 and 10 is considered normal. Despite the acronym, the test is named after Dr Virginia Apgar.

APH – Antepartum haemorrhage: CO bleeding beyond 24 weeks of pregnancy. Sometimes (but very rarely) called prepartum haemorrhage.

Arrest of descent: when your BT hasn't moved down into the birth canal during active labour, despite contractions and your CO pushing.

Arrest of dilatation/failure to progress: when your CO's cervix does not dilate to 10 cm (the dilation needed for your BT to be born) despite active labour.

B

Baby blues: in the days following birth, your CO's hormone levels will change dramatically and this, together with exhaustion and all of the emotions around childbirth, may lead her to feel weepy and/or irritable and 'down' after giving birth. These are known as the 'baby blues' and last a few days. See 'Post-natal depression' for symptoms that may require medical support.

Birth canal: your CO's uterus and vagina, through which your BT will pass when they are born.

Birth plan: a plan for how you and your CO would like the birth to go, including pain relief and where your CO would like to give birth.

Bloody show/show: when your CO passes a reddish brown mucus (also called a mucus plug) that has been sealing and protecting the cervix. A sign that your CO's body is getting ready for labour.

Braxton Hicks: practise contractions that your CO may experience throughout pregnancy. They do not dilate (i.e. open) the cervix and therefore they are completely safe. When they last for a long time and/or feel intense, they are sometimes described as false labour.

Br – Breech: when your BT is positioned bottom or feet first (rather than head down, or anterior) for birth. This is totally normal, but if your BT doesn't turn to be head first (which is the preferred position needed for birth) your CO's doctor may decide to turn the baby by hand. This is called external cephalic version (ECV).

C

Caesarean/C-section: when your BT is not delivered vaginally, but instead through an incision in your CO's abdomen and uterus. This is a surgical procedure and your CO will be given an epidural to remove any pain.

CEPH – Cephalic: when your BT is lying head down in the uterus.

Contraction: the regular tightening and relaxing of the uterine muscle – the largest muscle in your CO's body – to dilate, or open, the cervix, which is closed during pregnancy. Once the cervix is open, your BT can go through the birth canal and be born.

Crowning: when your BT's head remains visible without slipping back as your CO pushes during birth, ready for the final push to deliver your BT.

CTG – cardiotocograph: a recording of your BT's heartbeat. Can be used before labour to check heart rate and also during labour to see how your BT is responding to each contraction.

D

Dilate: to open. Used to describe how wide your CO's cervix has opened. 10 cm is the maximum and it is said that your CO is fully dilated at this point.

Doppler: a fetal monitor that amplifies the sound of your BT's heartbeat so that you and your CO can hear it.

Due date: the date your BT is expected to deploy. Pregnancy normally lasts 40 weeks, but babies born beyond 37 weeks are not considered early. Babies can also be late and if your CO or BT shows signs of distress, the birth could be induced.

E

Early or latent labour: the first part of the first stage of labour, when your CO's cervix dilates from 0–4 cm (her uterus will not be fully dilated until it is 10 cm).

Ectopic pregnancy: when your BT starts to develop outside your CO's uterus, usually in the Fallopian tube. Your CO will need an operation to remove the tube and pregnancy.

ECV – External cephalic version: when a doctor turns your BT by hand, in order to get them in the preferred position for birth (head down). Offered if your BT is in a breech position. This can be offered from 36 weeks. It will take place in hospital as your CO will need to have medication to make the muscles of her uterus relax and your BT will need to have their heartbeat monitored throughout.

EDD/EDC: expected date of delivery. See 'Due date' above.

Effacing or Effacement: thinning. Used to describe the cervix (neck of the womb) thinning ready for labour.

Electronic fetal monitor: used during delivery to record your BT's heartbeat and your CO's contractions.

Embryo: your BT in their very early stages of development (less than 10 weeks). After 10 weeks, your BT will be referred to as a foetus.

ENG – Engaged: your BT has moved into the preferred position for birth, with their head dropping down into your CO's pelvis.

Epidural: an anaesthetic injected into the small of your CO's back during labour to make her numb from the waist down.

Episiotomy: a cut made in the perineum (the skin between your CO's vagina and the anus) to enable better access to your BT by medical staff. It is needed for assisted birth. Your CO will need to be stitched up after delivery.

F

False labour: unlike true labour, false labour doesn't open your CO's cervix and the contractions don't grow consistently longer, stronger or closer together.

Fetus/Foetus: medical term for your BT before they are born.

FH – Fetal heart: used by your midwife to indicate they have heard your BT's heartbeat. Related terms include:

FHH: fetal heart heard

FHNH: fetal heart not heard (not the same as there being no heartbeat – just that it wasn't heard)

FMF: fetal movements felt

FMNF: fetal movements not felt

Free: refers to how much of your BT's head is 'engaged' (i.e. 'dropped') into your CO's pelvis. Free means that your BT's head is above your CO's pelvis.

Full term: a BT between 37 and 41 weeks.

Fundal height: the length between the top of your CO's uterus and her pubic bone. Measuring this can help date how far into pregnancy your CO is, and assess the growth of your BT.

Fundus: the top of the uterus (womb).

G

GDM – Gestational diabetes: a type of diabetes that some women develop during pregnancy. Diabetes is a condition where there is too much glucose in the blood. Your CO may require medical support.

Gestation: the time it takes your BT to grow until fully developed (usually 40 weeks).

Gestational hypertension: high blood pressure.

H

HB – Haemoglobin: an indication of iron levels in the blood. If this is too low, it may indicate that your CO has anaemia.

HG – Hyperemesis gravidarum: very severe form of nausea and vomiting, which can be very serious. It needs specialist treatment, sometimes in hospital.

Hypertension: high blood pressure.

Hypotension: low blood pressure.

I

Induction: help getting your CO's labour started, also called 'being induced'. A midwife or doctor can help induce labour using a membrane sweep, pessary or a hormone drip.

L

Latching on: when your BT takes your CO's nipple correctly into their mouth to breastfeed.

Latent or early labour: the first part of the first stage of labour, when your CO's cervix dilates from 0–4 cm (her uterus will not be fully dilated until it is 10 cm).

LIE: refers to the position of your BT in the uterus. You may also see Long Lie or LL, all of which mean longitudinal lie (vertical).

Lightening: BT dropping low into your CO's pelvis, ready for birth.

Linea nigra: a brown line of pigmentation that may develop on your CO's abdomen between the belly button and pubic area during pregnancy.

LOA – Left occiput anterior: relates to the position of your BT. LOA means that your BT is lying head down, with their back against your CO's left side.

Long/longitudinal. Refers to the position of your BT (vertical) in the uterus.

LOP – Left occiput posterior: relates to the position of your BT. LOP means that your BT is lying head down, with their head against the left-hand side of your CO's back.

M

Membrane sweep: when your CO's doctor or midwife uses their finger to 'sweep' the neck of your CO's womb to try to separate the membranes from her cervix. This is a method used to kick-start labour

Monochorionic: where more than one BT shares a placenta.

Multigravida: a CO who has had at least one pregnancy before.

Multipara/multip: a woman who has given birth at least once before.

N

NAD – Nothing abnormal detected: written when the doctor or midwife finds no problems.

Natural or normal birth: an unmedicated birth, without painkillers.

NE, NEng, Not Eng – Not engaged: refers to how much of your BT's head is 'engaged' (i.e. 'dropped') into your CO's pelvis. If your BT's head is not engaged, this means that it is still above your BT's pelvis.

NT scan – Nuchal translucency scan: a screening test to assess the likelihood of your BT having Down's syndrome. This is a non-invasive test, done during an ultrasound scan, that measures the fluid under the skin at the back of your BT's neck. Sometimes called a nuchal fold scan.

O

Obl – Oblique: refers to the position of your BT in the uterus. Oblique means that they are lying diagonally.

Oedema: fluid retention, which causes swelling in your CO's ankles, fingers and elsewhere.

P

Palpation: when the midwife or doctor feels your BT by moving their hands over your CO's abdomen.

PGO – stands for 'Protein, glucose, other': used to record the results of the urine tests she has at every antenatal appointment.

PGP – pregnancy-related pelvic girdle pain/SPD – Symphysis pubis dysfunction: uncomfortable symptoms caused by a misalignment or stiffness of your CO's pelvic joints at either the back or front of her pelvis. It's not harmful for your BT, but can be very painful for your CO. It's common, but severity can vary widely.

Pica: a pregnancy craving for non-food items, such as ice, coffee grounds and ashes. Please encourage your CO to talk to your midwife or doctor if she is craving non-food items, as some (not ice) are potentially harmful to her and your BT.

PIH – Pregnancy-induced hypertension or gestational hypertension: high blood pressure.

Placenta/umbilical cord: your BT's life support system– the organ that connects your CO to your BT and through which they receive nutrients and oxygen. Your CO will deliver the placenta after the birth of your BT and it will then be termed the afterbirth.

Placental abruption: when the placenta partially or completely separates from the uterus (womb) before your BT is delivered.

Placenta praevia – also known as low-lying placenta: when the placenta is in the lower area of the uterus and is covering part or all of the cervix, effectively blocking your BT's exit route. Most likely to result in a Caesarean birth.

Posterior position: refers to the position of your BT in the uterus. The back of your BT's head is towards your CO's back.

Post-natal: after the birth.

Postnatal depression: depression that occurs after the deployment of your BT. While it is common to feel a little down after birth – sometimes referred to as 'baby blues' – if this is prolonged or chronic, speak to your medical support team.

Pre-eclampsia: a potentially serious condition characterised by the onset of high blood pressure (where blood pressure was previously normal) and protein in the urine.

Prenatal: before the birth of your BT.

Presentation: the position of your BT – the part of their body 'presenting' will be born first.

Preterm/premature: before the full term of the pregnancy is complete, e.g. earlier than 37 weeks

Primigravida: a CO pregnant for the first time.

Primipara (Prim/Primip): a CO giving birth for the first time.

Prot – Protein: refers to your CO's urine test and whether protein has been found. Plus signs (+) are used to indicate the levels of protein found, with three being the highest level. Nil means no protein was found and Tr means a trace of protein has been found.

Proteinuria: protein in your CO's urine.

Q

Quickening: the first movements of your BT that your CO can feel. May feel like a fluttering, or a bubbling, inside.

R

ROA – Right occiput anterior: relates to the position of your BT in the uterus. ROA means that your BT is lying head down, with their back against your CO's right side.

Rooting/rooting reflex: your BT will instinctively search for your CO's breast to feed and the rooting reflex consists of head turning and sucking movements.

ROP – Right occiput posterior: refers to the position of your BT in the uterus. In this case, it means your BT is lying head down, with their head against the right-hand side of your CO's back.

S

Show: while your CO is pregnant, the cervix is sealed shut with a mucus plug. Just before labour starts, or in early labour, your CO's cervix will open and the plug will come away. Your CO may see this 'show' as a pink (or brown) jelly-like substance. Some COs do not know they have lost the plug and do not have a show.

Sonogram/ultrasound: a procedure that uses high-frequency sound waves to create an image of your unborn BT. Can help date how far into pregnancy your CO is and assess the growth of your BT.

SPD – Symphysis pubis dysfunction/PGP – pregnancy-related pelvic girdle pain: uncomfortable symptoms caused by a misalignment or stiffness of your CO's pelvic joints at either the back or front of her pelvis. It's not harmful for your BT, but can be very painful for your CO. It's common, but severity can vary widely.

SROM – Spontaneous rupture of membranes: when your CO's waters break naturally when she's full term and in labour.

Stages of labour: labour is divided into three stages. The first stage leads up to the actual birth and has three phases: early labour, active labour and the transitional phase. The second stage is when your CO delivers your BT. The third stage is when your CO delivers the placenta, or afterbirth (your BT's life support system for the past nine months).

T

Term: the amount of time it takes a BT to fully develop – 37–42 weeks.

Tr – Transverse: refers to the position of your BT in the uterus. Transverse means that they are lying across your CO's body and if your BT cannot be turned, a Caesarean will be required.

Trimester: the word trimester means 'three months'. Pregnancy is broken down into three trimesters – three periods of three months – the first, second and third trimesters.

Triple test: a blood test that may indicate the probability of chromosomal abnormalities. It will not determine whether your BT will definitely be affected, but will help you and your CO decide if you wish to have a diagnostic (invasive) test to be certain. Three substances in your CO's blood are measured – Alpha-fetoprotein (AFP), Unconjugated estriol (UE) and Human chorionic gonadotropin (hCG) – hence the name 'triple test.'

U

Ultrasound scan/sonogram: a procedure that uses high-frequency sound waves to create an image of your unborn BT. Can help date how far into pregnancy your CO is and assess the growth of your BT.

Umbilical cord/placenta: your BT's life support system – the organ that connects your CO to your BT and through which they receive nutrients and oxygen. Your CO will deliver the placenta after the birth of your BT, and it will then be termed the afterbirth.

Uterus: a medical term for the womb, where your BT grows.

V

VE: vaginal examination.

Ventouse: a vaccum that may be used to help deliver your BT. A suction cup is put onto your BT's head to help guide them out.

Vernix caseosa: a white, waxy substance that develops around your BT to protect their skin from amniotic fluid. It is absorbed into your BT's skin shortly after birth.

VX – Vertex: the crown (top) of your BT's head.

W

Waters breaking: this is when the bag of fluid that has surrounded and protected your BT – the amniotic sac – breaks and the fluid leaks out. It can be either a trickle or a gush. If your CO's waters break before labour starts, phone your midwife. Without amniotic fluid, your BT is less protected from infection.

Z

Zygote: a fertilised egg – the start of your BT.

Index